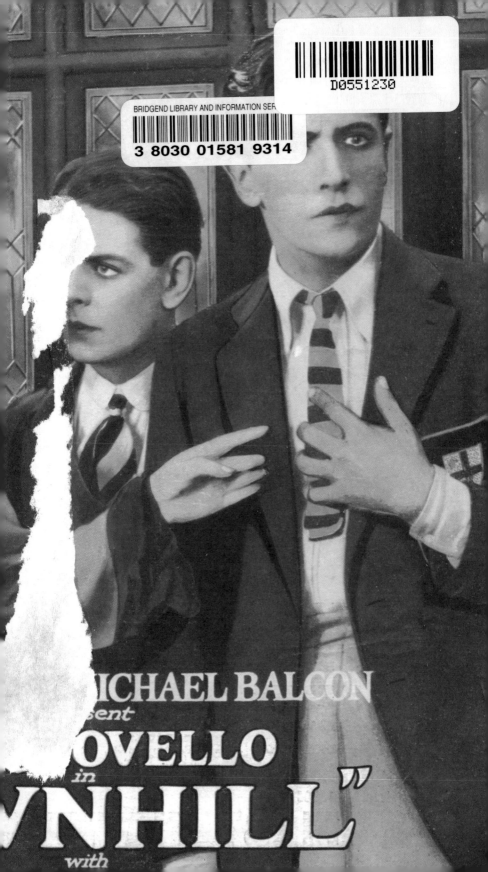

ICHAEL BALCON
sent
OVELLO
in
VNHILL"
with

Ivor Novello

Portrait of a Star

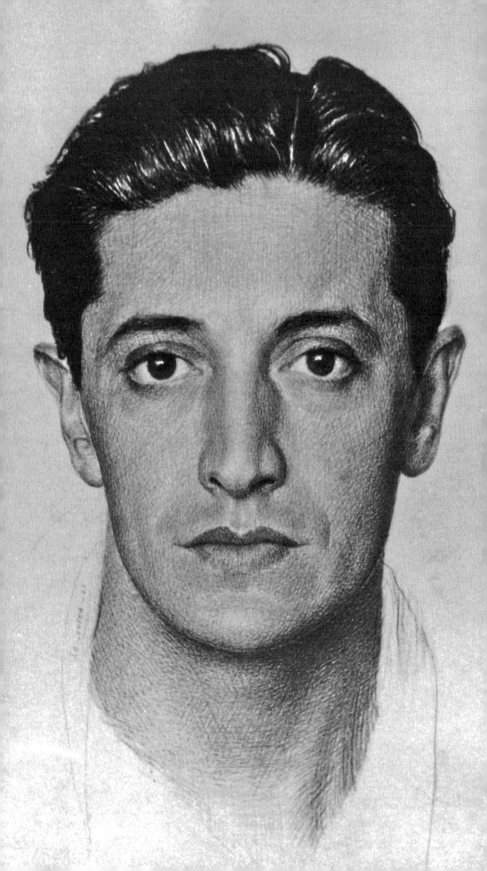

Ivor Novello

Portrait of a Star

Paul Webb

HAUS
BOOKS
London

Originally published under the title Ivor Novello
– A Portrait of a Star by Paul Webb
© Paul Webb 1999, Stage Directions

This revised edition is published in Great Britain in 2005
by Haus Publishing Limited
26 Cadogan Court
London SW3 3BX

The moral right of the author has been asserted

A CIP catalogue record for this book
is available from the British Library

ISBN 1-904950-48-5

Designed and typeset by Rick Fawcett

Printed and bound by Graphicom, Vicenza, Italy

Front cover: Mander and Mitchinson

Back cover: Mander and Mitchinson

www.hauspublishing.com

CONTENTS

For Adam
(1963-1995)

ACKNOWLEDGEMENTS

A great many people have been enormously helpful in the course of my researching and writing this book. First I would like to thank John Bedding and Paul Taylor of Samuel French, acting on behalf of the Trustees of the Novello Estate, for giving permission to quote from copyright material, to Sir Thomas Arnold for his permission to quote from *The Dancing Years*, and Barbara Schwepcke and Robert Pritchard of Haus Publishing. I am very grateful to Sheridan Morley for permission from the Trustees of the Coward Estate to reproduce copyright material, and for his knowledge of theatrical history, especially that relating to his grandmother, Gladys Cooper.

I have traced, where possible, copyright holders for permission to use the photographs featured in this book. Any omissions will be rectified in future editions. Meanwhile I would like to thank Mark Fox, archivist of the Really Useful Theatres collection, the PA News Photo Library, the National Portrait Gallery, Richard Mangan of the Mander and Mitchenson Collection, John Snelson, John Entwistle of Reuters, and the staff of the Corporation of London's Shoe Lane Library.

Among Ivor's co-stars and colleagues who provided insights into and memories of Ivor's career were Mary Ellis, Roma Beaumont, Jessica James and Muriel Barron, and I am particularly grateful to Gordon Duttson, Ivor's last private secretary and close friend. Elspeth March, Geoffrey Toone, and Eva Norman (Minnie Rayner's niece) were among many friends of Ivor's who also shared their memories.

Peter Wilcox, ex-General Manager of the Aldwych Theatre, proved to be a mine of theatre information and enthusiasm.

A FUNERAL AS FOREWORD

In the twentieth century there were three funerals (leaving aside those of reigning monarchs) that saw spectacularly large crowds turn out to express their sense of loss at the passing of an icon.

Churchill's in 1965 was a mark of respect for a long life of public service, an indomitable will that rallied the nation in the face of seemingly overwhelming odds and a superb sense of oratory that both expressed and strengthened the mood of the British people at their most critical point. Diana, Princess of Wales was mourned for a life cut tragically short, and as a great beauty with a particular brand of glamour that combined the ageless appeal of royalty with that of a super-model, while carrying out the medieval healing role of the crown in the twentieth century context of AIDS and landmines.

The third was that of Ivor Novello, a man whose name is now vaguely remembered as the composer of lush nostalgic tunes, largely relegated to *Friday Night is Music Night* from the Golders Green Hippodrome. Yet the size of the crowds that turned out for his funeral service at the Golders Green Crematorium on a cold March morning in 1951, recorded for posterity on Pathé newsreel, is evidence of the enormous popular appeal that his work had on the British public for five decades, and the unrivalled personal affection in which he was held, by those he worked with as well as those for whom he performed on stage and screen.

In industries where jealousy and spite are the vampire teeth behind the velvet lips of luvviedom, Ivor Novello stood out for his kindness. 'Kind' is the phrase most frequently used of him by those with whom he worked, while his memorial plaque in the actor's church, St Paul's Covent Garden, describes him in a Shakespearean quote as 'The dearest friend, the kindest man, the best condition'd and unwearied spirit in doing courtesies.'

The fact that another memorial plaque (one of several to him) is located in St Paul's Cathedral is further evidence of his position as a leading figure in British theatre and film, but that the memorial to a man famous for his beauty – according to Noël Coward "There are two perfect things in this world – my mind and Ivor's profile" – and for his determinedly theatrical lifestyle should be unveiled by the distinctly un-camp Group Captain Douglas Bader is evidence not just of the breadth of his appeal, but of the fact that his music and his shows (which he always insisted were plays with music rather than musicals) were as effective at expressing and bolstering public feeling in both world wars as Churchill's oratory or Bader's morale-boosting exploits.

For it is usually forgotten that it was Ivor who provided one of the most popular and poignant songs of the First World War – 'Keep the Home Fires Burning' – as well as the most beautiful song of the Second – 'We'll Gather Lilacs' – which perfectly expressed the war-weariness and longing for a peace that seemed, in 1944, to be finally in sight. These achievements alone should keep his name alive, but it is his versatility, the range as well as depth of his talent that makes his posthumous slide from fame all the more puzzling.

Famous and rich through a single song in 1914, he went on to become Britain's most popular male silent movie star in the 1920s, playing the lead in Alfred Hitchcock's first success, *The Lodger* (1926), was a West End matinee idol as an actor, and a commercial success as a playwright. From 1935 until his premature death, aged 58, in 1951, during a run of what many people considered his finest work, *King's Rhapsody*, he saved Drury Lane from closure and single-handedly kept British musical theatre alive, comfortably beating American imports like *Oklahoma!* in the battle of box office receipts.

The fact that royalty featured so heavily in his shows has been taken as a sign of how 'irrelevant' he must have been, and even to his contemporaries they sometimes seemed old fashioned, a throwback to the operettas that he had enjoyed so much as a teenager in the 1900s. Yet Royalty was an essential part of the society in which Ivor lived and for which he wrote. King George V's Jubilee (in which *Glamorous Night* was first performed, and which the King and Queen Mary attended), the Abdication Crisis and the subsequent promotion of the new Royal Family – particularly the public obsession with Princesses Elizabeth and Margaret Rose, whose picture can still be seen pasted onto a wall in the attic of Ann Frank's house in Amsterdam – were all of national and international relevance at the time he was composing his West End shows.

Even if some of the music he produced could be criticised as too derivative of all those Viennese confections that dominated musical theatre on both sides of the Atlantic until Show Boat broke all the rules in 1927, one must not forget, to quote his friend and rival Noël Coward again, that even 'cheap music' can be remarkably potent.

Ivor's music was never 'cheap', and at its best stands alongside Lehàr, Kern and Elgar, but it did connect to the public for which it was written. It spoke to them with eloquence and feeling, and was reciprocated by an affection and admiration that has never been equalled.

The purpose of this book is to resurrect interest in, and appreciation of, his career, setting him in the theatrical, film, and social context of his time, and showing how he was a vastly more versatile and talented man than he is currently given credit for. His appeal cut across the normal demarcation lines, and spanned the chasm between young gay men who wanted to be him, shop-girls who wanted to marry him (an ambition shared – equally hopelessly – by his most glamorous co-star, Gladys Cooper), middle aged and older women who wanted to mother or mother-in-law him and war heroes like Bader who found his music both an escape from, and a buttressing against the horrors of combat. Given this, and given, too, the late twentieth century's obsession with male physical beauty, and the cult of celebrity, it is all more bizarre that so few people are aware of Ivor Novello, and that when it comes to the epitome of male glamour from the 1920s and 1930s, the only role model the public remember is Noël Coward.

10

To be fair, even Noël, one of the few men (another being Oscar Wilde) who embodies a style as well as a personality, has been partially by-passed by teenage culture. Going into a well-known record shop in the early 1990s I asked an Australian assistant where I might find CDs by Noël Coward. She stopped chewing gum for a moment to ask, in an uninterested tone, "Who are they?" If Sir Noël Coward can be mistaken for a 1990s pop group then perhaps it is not entirely surprising that Ivor Novello tends to be enjoyed by those, like amateur operatic companies, with a specialised love of musical theatre, rather than the wider British – and American – public. As the twentieth century's first superstar, at the top of both the stage and screen professions, and with a devoted fan following to match, Ivor Novello deserves better.

Ivor and Mam (Clara Novello Davies) c 1903

LARGER-THAN-LIFE MOTHER

The most important influence in Ivor's life was his mother. In later years those outside his closest circle of friends could not understand how he forbore her eccentricities, her frequent requests for large sums of money, and, above all, her drinking. Elspeth March recalled how guests at Ivor's country house, Redroofs, would have to sneak out of the house and across Littlewick Green to the village pub in order to stock up on supplies of alcohol, which was a banned substance whenever his mother, known to all as Mam, was visiting.

Clara Novello Davies was a Welsh girl whose father, Jacob Davies, had been a miner with a superb singing voice. His dark good looks were classically Welsh, but Clara liked to fantasise that they came from a more exotic source:

'His shining black curls, handsome flashing eyes and olive complexion bore out the suggestion that in Wales there is to be found a strong Spanish strain, whose ancestry on the distaff side apparently extended a most cordial welcome to the rescued members of the ill-fated Armada.'

It was this combination of voice and dark good looks that had won the heart of the local minister's daughter, Margaret Evans. Unfortunately, the minister disapproved, so the couple had to elope. When Clara was born, her father insisted on naming her after Clara Novello, a leading Italian singer whose voice he greatly admired, much to the fury of the child's grandfather, who refused to pronounce such a heathen name at the Christening ceremony. Jacob was forced to name her himself, a Napoleonic touch that one cannot help feeling appealed to Mam's dramatic imagination and rather romantic view of her life and career.

Indeed, she seemed to feel that she and the late Emperor were soul-mates. A woman who liked to get her own way, she once wrote 'I have always loved conquest, and the greater the obstacle in my path the greater has been my determination to overcome it.'

Developing her theme, she continued: 'Like Napoleon, for me there have been "no Alps", for in all my high hopes I have had a higher faith that made me ignore alpine altitudes as mere mole hills in the way of my objective. Strangely enough, on my first outing in my mother's arms, she was stopped by a gypsy woman who peered into my small face and told her that Napoleon was my "guide".'

Whatever higher power may have been looking after her, on earth the dominant figure in her life was her father. Determined to convey his love of music to his daughter, he was delighted to discover that she had considerable natural talent, growing up to be a precociously gifted girl who supplemented the family's income as a piano and singing teacher. Her father's affection had a similar intensity to that of Mr Barrett of Wimpole Street for his daughter, Elizabeth, and he used emotional blackmail to keep Clara at home, even when she was old enough to make her own way in the world. As she later recalled:

'My own voice had developed greatly under father's careful tuition, and the manager of a touring opera company approached him in regard to allowing me to accept an engagement, but was met with a flat refusal. I was rather keen on the idea, but all thought of it left me when father said: "Go with them, Clara, and you are lost to me forever."'

Clara had a tendency towards the fuller figure, even as a girl, but with her dark good looks, extrovert personality and boundless self-confidence, she soon attracted the attentions of the local boys. In her autobiography, *The Life I Have Loved* (1940), Clara describes in some detail her courtship with David Davies (no relation – or not a close one, at any rate), a

14

good looking and decent but rather dull young man, several years older than her.

He was, in many ways, her opposite, but this was a large part of his attraction: 'I always think it was this solidity in him, so unlike my volatile self, that drew me closer to Dave, who was solid as the Rock of Gibraltar.'

Known to her family for several years, and a member of the choir that Clara's father ran, he had fallen for Clara when she was still a child, and stated his intention of marrying when she grew up. Her mother was indignant – "I'll never be mother-in-law to you, Dave Davies" – and even when Clara was of an age for such romantic ideas, both parents were less than keen on Dave as a life partner for their daughter.

David had more than his future mother-in-law's caprice to contend with – Clara was quite happy to play him off against other suitors, including a swell of a cousin from London. Reading her account of these skirmishes some fifty years after they took place, her girlish pleasure in the allure and power of her femininity comes across strongly, but so does the less beguiling streak of ruthless self-centredness, and male readers, at any rate, will be appalled at the way she merrily rode roughshod over David's emotions.

Eventually even he had had enough, and, hailing a horse-drawn cab – which, given his disinclination for making dramatic gestures, should have warned her that something was up – he gave her an ultimatum: she would have to accept or reject his proposal of marriage, once and for all – and they were going to stay in the cab until he got an answer. Although she was being proposed to behind a horse rather than swept off onto one, Clara was sufficiently impressed to accept. She was gaining a husband but, given his surname, she was able to keep hers (no need to change her business stationery) and was marrying a man who, if played right, she could bend to her will. Whatever the mores of the time, and despite this one case of him putting his foot down, it was always clear who would wear the trousers in their household.

Even at their wedding, however, he played second fiddle, for her heart still belonged to Daddy, who had made terrible scenes

15

over the loss of his daughter to another man. On the wedding day, 31 October 1883, she gave a public display of affection to her father than makes one cringe on Dave's behalf:

'At last the ring was on my finger, and Dave kept whispering that he must have the first kiss, but I whisked my veil up smartly in father's direction, and the bridal kiss was his, as I felt it should be.'

Both David and Clara wanted children. Their first was a girl, Myfanwy Margaret, who died in infancy. Both parents were distraught, naturally, and when they had their second and last child, their love for him had an extra edge. Clara transformed herself into Mam during the pregnancy, and waited for the birth with an unassailable conviction that it would be a boy. Other than the sex, she had two further requests for Fate. One was that the baby should be beautiful, the other was that he would grow up to become a composer. All three of her wishes were to be granted, though not in their entirety. The baby was a boy, but he was not, as they would have said at the time, 'the marrying kind' so Mam never had the grand-children she would have loved to have doted on. He was to become the most famously beautiful man in British theatrical history, but those looks would blind contemporary and later critics to his artistic achievements, and he was indeed to become a composer, but his greatest love was not the piano or the music sheet but the stage, and he was to write musicals – or, more accurately, and in his preferred term, musical plays – rather than the classical music on which Mam had pinned her hopes.

When Ivor entered the world, on 15 January 1893, his mother's first reaction was negative. The dark-haired baby had a pronounced and prolonged nose, which made a mockery of her expectations of beauty. Amused relatives compared it to that of his uncle Ebeneezer, whose own nose was a by-word for size and distinction. Mam found this far from entertaining, but her hormones overcame her horror and she took the baby to her heart as well as her breast. As it happened, Ivor rapidly 'grew into' his nose, and became a strikingly attractive child, developing into a stunning young man whose looks could bring conversations to a halt in smart restaurants as he arrived to take his seat at a strategically-placed table. More will be said about these looks later, but it is important to acknowledge, at this early stage, that his physical beauty was an essential ingredient in the charm and personality that captivated his friends, colleagues and public throughout his life.

By the time Ivor was born, Mam was not only a singing teacher but in charge of the formidable Welsh Ladies Choir. Ivor may have been the ultimate expression of her one-woman *Triumph of the Will*, but in the meantime she needed another outlet for her energy. Although in later life her choir was to be something of a joke, in the 1890s it was the most successful of its kind in Wales, and not long after Ivor's birth she took it across the Atlantic to Chicago, to sing in the World Fair.

The trans-Atlantic element to Ivor's career was heavily influenced by Mam's own travels, and by the fact that her reputation was to be as strong in New York as it was in Cardiff, the city where she and David brought up Ivor. On her return from Chicago she found her baby son had transferred his affections to the wet nurse who had been left in charge of him. Mam clasped him dramatically to her bosom until the child showed an appropriate degree of pleasure at being back in the maternal embrace.

Once he had been reclaimed, she immediately detected in him the signs of an infant prodigy, even in his wailing: 'I can remember the funny way in which he used to cry, in perfect thirds, which were not at all inharmonious to listen to.'

Mam and David christened the boy David Ivor Davies, but he was always known as Ivor – not least to distinguish him from his father. Although Ivor inherited his love of, and talent for, music from his mother, together with her Italianate colouring, pictures of him as an adult with his parents clearly show that some of his looks came from his un-glamorous but handsome father.

David's good looks proved to be of advantage to his wife's career when her Welsh Ladies Choir received a command to perform before Queen Victoria at Osborne House, on the Isle of Wight. Mam's memoir recalls the fact that the Queen liked her whisky – wags have suggested that Prince Albert, weary of his matrimonial duties at night, encouraged her to drink before retiring for the night and thus left her not only a widow but a solitary drinker. Whatever the reason for the drink in hand, it was clear that the ageing Queen still had an eye for the gentlemen, and when Mam

Ivor with his parents, David and Clara, early 1930s

was presented to Her Majesty after the performance, the Queen was heard to observe "You have a very handsome husband, Mrs Davies!" This subsequently produced much amusement among the ladies of the choir and a blushing response from David, but whether it was his looks or Mam's music that clenched the matter, the Queen decided to award the title Royal Welsh Ladies Choir. In addition, she gave Mam a brooch, in the form of her monogram, VRI – 'Victoria. Regina. Imperatrix.' In a move that foreshadowed that of an E F Benson character with the insignia of the MBE, Mam took to wearing the Queen-Empress' brooch day and night.

This is the one recorded event where David may, however unwittingly, have contributed to Mam's professional success. Normally he simply got on with his job – in the Rates department at Cardiff Council. Even here, Mam rather than David had been the driving force. The job had become vacant, and was in the gift of a local politician. No-one promoted his interests or supported his candidacy with as much histrionic vigour and charm as Mam, who was rewarded with a job that kept her husband usefully and modestly employed for the rest of his life. When, on occasion, he ventured to suggest that young Ivor might have more reliable prospects in local government than in music, his comments were treated with withering contempt and the unspoken assumption that if Mam had arranged her husband's career he was in no position to object to her arranging their son's.

Mam often worked from home, so Ivor grew up in a house filled with music. One of the cultural centres of Cardiff, it was visited by nearly all of the most important singers of the day, for whom Cardiff was a major venue, and Mam a local figure of influence as well as hospitality. She may have been a classic case of the 'stage mother' in her determination to promote her child's career, but although she conformed to some of the stereotypes of this well-documented phenomenon she was atypical in two crucial ways. The first is that she saw Ivor on the conductor's podium, controlling an orchestra that would be playing his own composition in an opera house – not for her the smell of greasepaint and green-room romances. The second, and more important in the short term, was that unlike similarly ambitious mothers, who classically lived their own thwarted ambitions through their progeny (and Mrs

Coward is a striking example of this) Mam had a successful career of her own, and was able – indeed, determined – to open every professional door she could for her son.

A childish taste for wearing his mother's clothes was a reflection not only of his love of dressing up for its own sake, and a youthful penchant for drag – there is a striking photograph of him dressed as an Edwardian pin-up girl when he was in his early teens – but of the fact that this was an age when colour and glamour belonged almost exclusively to women. In addition to the already overpowering presence of his mother, larger than life and than her dressmaker would have liked, there were a stream of beautiful and talented women through the Davies household, of whom Clara Butt was perhaps the best known, and one of young Ivor's closest friends and admirers.

Ivor was page boy at Clara Butt's wedding to Kennerley Rumford, and years later he recalled the event in a newspaper interview:

'Dressed in a white satin frock, I made myself thoroughly ill with strawberry ices ten minutes before the ceremony. Outside the church someone said, "Look at that darling little angel!". At that precise moment I was trying to check an irresistible urge to be horribly sick.'

Even at this stage he attracted admiration – not just for his looks and as the only child of the household, but because of a talent for moving an audience to tears through music: partly his technical ability as a singer, partly through a projection of his personality, partly through his talent as a performer, but largely because of his total belief and involvement in the emotions he was expressing. This combination, which was to make him a West End sensation and the most successful figure in British popular culture for thirty years, was already there, in embryo form, in Cathedral Road, Cardiff.

A particular example of Ivor's charm in action was recalled, years later, by his junior school teacher, Mrs McCrory, who described how the angelic looking child, with perfect skin, vast brown eyes and an engaging manner sang a sentimental ballad called 'Tatters' at the end of term concert. By the time he had finished not only was there not a dry eye in the house, but grown men and women were sobbing.

Ivor Novello in a school production c.1908

Similarly, at a singing competition at the National Eisteddford, the judge, speaking to a moist-eyed audience after Ivor had finished, said: 'You have just listened to an angel singing and I think I am right in saying he has taken us all before the throne of Grace.' The little angel had disguised himself in girl's clothes in order to enter the competition, and when his deception was revealed the judges decided to give him a special prize.

Ivor enjoyed performing, whether in public, as a pageboy at Clara Butt's wedding, or in private, singing songs with Adelina Patti when she visited Mam at home. He accompanied Mam to London, where she had established a studio in Maida Vale, and on these trips made his first visits to the West End, beginning – appropriately and fatefully – with the Theatre Royal, Drury Lane.

His interest in theatre had begun, in the traditional way for Edwardian children, with the gift of a toy theatre, which Mam had bought for him. She recalled that 'it became the joy of his young life...Dolls were bought in numbers, and suitable 'casts' were formed after certain flaxen and brunette beauties had their hair 'bobbed' and became 'heroes' and 'villains' accordingly.'

His childhood experience of Drury Lane, the long climb up the stairs to the gallery, the vastness of the auditorium and the magic of the stage, made an enormous impression on him, though Mam may have been tingeing her recollections with the benefit of hindsight when she recalled that 'he told me, in later years, the thought that flashed into his mind ... 'some day I am going to make a play with music, a great big play, and be in it myself on that stage.'

He liked to record his impressions of glamorous actresses, and imaginary plays of his own in which they took the lead roles, but the means for recording these memories and fantasies were sometimes inappropriate. Weighed in the balance, theatre took priority over everything, including expensive presents:

'Mr Lloyd George was a family friend, and to me a sort of fairy uncle...one day he gave me a set of Robert Louis Stevenson, with his name and mine on each of the fly leaves. Alas, I was possessed with a passion for drawing, and could never lay my hands on enough scribbling paper: so the blank pages were irresistible.

One by one I tore them out, and covered them with the profiles of imaginary beauties; *Kidnapped* is the only one that remains intact.'

Mam complemented his informal cultural experiences with musical lessons at Gloucester, but if he were to become a great composer, he would need the best education available. Accordingly, she decided to enter him for a choral scholarship at Magdalen College Choir School. In the only known occasion during their entire married life in which he defied her, David hid the entry form from Mam in a chest of drawers.

Mam only discovered the subterfuge when it was, technically, too late. Not letting mere formalities get in the way of Ivor's career, and with an audacity that puts Mrs Coward – and even Mrs Garland – to shame, she hurtled up to Oxford with Ivor in his best clothes, and demanded that the rules be waived for a child of such obvious talent. The bemused board at Magdalen agreed, and even re-arranged the audition schedule to fit in with Mam's. Ivor auditioned – and won the scholarship. Although only ten, his professional career had begun.

Ivor and Mam, 1st World War

ADOLESCENCE

Ivor's time at Magdalen was an entirely happy one. He loved the architecture and the atmosphere of Oxford. It was, to a sensitive boy with a sense of history as well as of beauty, a magical place. Some forty years later, Evelyn Waugh wrote *Brideshead Revisited*, in which he immortalised the Oxford of the 1920s, which he remembered, and celebrated, as a lost paradise, a secret garden behind a wall to which, for a while, he had the key. Yet even in the 1920s there was a sense of loss, a recognition that a way of life had passed for ever with the Great War, that things were not as elegant, or carefree, as they had been.

Ivor was fortunate enough to have experienced Oxford at its peak, in the golden afternoon of Edwardian England. The chapel, the cloisters, the honey-coloured college buildings, the immaculately kept lawns, the college servants, the undergraduates conscious of being part of a legacy of centuries of privileged youth, all helped create the impression of, to quote from Shakespeare's Richard II an 'other Eden, demi-paradise.'

It was Oxford, as much as Heidelberg or any of the other settings for the operettas that he so enjoyed as a teenager, that helped create an image of a better, more glamorous world that he would bring to life on stage. That Oxford was as gorgeous as he remembered, that life was as elegant and pampered in Edwardian England as Merchant Ivory films suggest, was undeniable.

True, Edwardian England was racked with crises – over the House of Lords, the Budget, Social Security, Ireland – and there were waves of strikes that polarised public opinion, and scares about possible German invasion plans. There was a level of poverty that would be considered intolerable today, and Sufragettes were making violent protests about women's right to vote, and being force-fed in prison. Yet these problems existed alongside enormous privilege, and for those who were young, talented, healthy, and well-off, life was comfortable, charming and confident, in a way that, after 1914, could never be recreated.

From 1903 to 1909 he was able to wallow in his enjoyment of Oxford life. A letter home combined his enjoyment of the music he performed with a childish interest in less rarefied pleasures: and a taste for theatrical terms of endearment that was to become more pronounced as he grew older.

My Darling Mam,

I am singing two very big solos on Sunday night next. You must – Dr Roberts says you can – come up in the organ pew with him. He is awfully pleased with me. I have sung two solos and one verse part 'As Pants the Hart' (Spohr), 'Lord God of Heaven and Earth' (Spohr's 'Last Judgement') and a verse from Garret.

I want some grub badly – will you send me a big hamper with plenty of fruit and sweets, chocolate, cakes, shortbread biscuits, potted meat and jams?

> *Goodbye,*
> *Beauty,*
> *Popsy,*
> *Darling,*
> *Love,*
> *Ivor.*

Ivor's choral career came to an abrupt, but suitably cinematic, end in 1909, when he was sixteen. For some time he it had been fashionable to go to Magdalen on a Sunday evening to hear the dark-haired chorister with the sweet, soaring voice. The chapel is still, as then, open to the public for evensong and Sunday services. In Ivor's time the organist and man in charge of the choir was a larger than life character, Varley Roberts, who was sufficiently admired in his own right to be caricatured in a 'Spy' cartoon. Ivor's attractions were of a different nature, and his last performance, of 'O, For the Wings of a Dove', was rapturously received by his lady and gentlemen admirers in the congregation. It was to prove a high note on which to end his career, for his voice broke the next morning. It was an inevitable blow, but a bitter one, nonetheless.

26

His time at Oxford is relatively forgotten now, but it was of fundamental importance not only for the musical training that it gave him, but, more importantly, for the urge to perform before an audience.

Mam had, as usual, got her way in sending him to Oxford, but, as was often the case, her wishes were only partially answered. He had indeed been set on the road to a musical career, but he had also been given a taste of the limelight, of the adrenaline that a public performance produced, the camaraderie of his fellow performers and the admiration of his chosen profession. In historical terms the Theatre had its origins in the Church, and so, it turned out, did Ivor.

For now, however, he was still under Mam's direction, which was a resolutely musical one. He went to study under Dr (later Sir Herbert) Brewer in Gloucester. This proved to be less than successful, and he left with Brewer's withering dismissal: "You have absolutely no future in music, Davies."

Brewer may have been a great organist but he was, in this case at least, a poor judge of character. Ivor was determined to prove him wrong, and eventually did so, spectacularly. This determination was a necessary ingredient in his later success, and beneath the easy charm and engaging smile, the boyish enthusiasm and famous inability to say anything unpleasant about any-one (or, at least, to qualify criticism with a compliment) was a hard-edged ambition and resolve that few people were allowed to see, but which informed and underpinned his professional life.

For the moment, however, he had still to prove himself. There was no question of his going to a normal school in order to round off his education, let alone take a conventional job. He had a ready-made outlet for his musical energy in Mam's work – she had moved her centre of operations from Maida Vale (telegraphic address 'Semibreve') to a studio in Hanover Square. While she was in London he took pupils in piano lessons at Cardiff, and as soon as he could he moved to London to join her – she took on a new flat near the studio so as not to waste valuable time travelling to work.

Ivor was, even in his teens, aware of the business side of an artist's life, and realised that he would be better able to concentrate on composing if someone with the appropriate skills looked after his business affairs. At the beginning of the 1909 tax year he wrote to a young accountant, Fred Allen, whom his mother had met, and began a life-long business association:

Dear Mr Allen,

Mother has told me you are going to be kind enough to look after my lucrative business! Will you be satisfied with 5 per cent. (whatever that may mean)? I can see you increasing your income by at least three-half-pence a year! I am enclosing a list of pupils, number of lessons and the times they come.

Yours,

Ivor Novello Davies.

As well as taking on pupils, he was getting on with the serious business of writing songs. He had an early start with 'Spring of the Year', published by Boosey and Hawkes, which had its first public airing at the Albert Hall. This suitably vast platform was also to be the scene of his first critical and commercial success, 'The Little Damosel' in 1910. It was quickly taken up by leading sopranos, including the redoubtable Madame Galli-Curci.

On the strength of the early efforts he was asked to write the score of a Pageant for a Festival of Empire that was being staged in Canada. Although the Pageant never materialised, his expenses to Canada were guaranteed, so he took the opportunity of travelling there, and of moving on to New York before returning to England.

He loved New York from the start, taking in as many shows as he could, before his finances forced a return home. He might never have reached England had it not been for a dog that he had bought in Montreal. He had booked his passage on a liner, the Empress of India, but on the day he should have sailed his dog disappeared. Refusing to leave without his pet, he cancelled his booking, and spent two days trying to track the animal down.

A concert booking in London meant that he had to give up the search, so he reluctantly booked himself on another ship, Pretorian. Two days out to sea Ivor received two cables:

'One stated that the Empress of India had been rammed in a fog and gone down in ten minutes; over 900 people had been drowned, among them poor Laurence Irving and Mabel

Hackney. The other cable was from my landlady in Montreal. My dog had turned up the day after I had left!'

London was where money and reputation were to be made, not Cardiff, so he and Mam increasingly spent their time there, while David held the fort back in Wales. In later years it was sometimes suggested that Ivor had deserted his Welsh roots, had written about English Lanes and Roses of England, had set his shows in China and Baltic Kingdoms, had had a weekend house in Berkshire and a holiday home in Jamaica, but never one in Wales.

This is, up to a point, a fair comment, though equally one could point to the fact that many of the Welsh celebrities one can think of – Emlyn Williams and Richard Burton, for example – left Wales to go where the acting work was. Even the Prince of Wales has no home in the land from which he takes his title. Why should Ivor have been any different?

London was where the theatres were, and around which the nascent British film industry developed. Gainsborough Pictures, for whom Ivor was to work for several years, was based in Islington. Ivor was a sun lover – sunshine was one of the few pleasures of his brief spell as a Hollywood screen writer in the 1930s – and Wales, for all its charm, its coastline and its mountains, its music and its people, comes a very poor second to the Caribbean when it comes to sunshine.

On the plus side, Ivor never lost his strongly Welsh accent, nor tried to, despite living in an age when regional accents were heavily frowned upon. For a leading actor on the British stage to retain a Welsh accent should be a sufficient mark of pride in his origins for the most nationalistic of his countrymen. Naturally his accent wasn't an issue when he was making silent movies, but when he made talkies he refused to compromise, which is why the Russian Prince Felix that he played on stage (1932) and screen (1933) in *I Lived With You* had an accent that was more Porthcawl than Petersburg.

London provided not only a professional launching-pad but an enormous amount of pleasure. He loved the theatre with a passion that few have rivalled, and spent all his spare time soaking up the best that Edwardian London had to offer. Although mechanised transport was being rapidly introduced, this was still an age of horse-drawn carriages, gaslight and Stage-Door Johnnies, of Gaiety Girls (named after one of London's most glamorous theatres, situated opposite the Strand Theatre in the Aldwych, and, appallingly, demolished to make way for an office block in the 1950s).

He saw all the most popular actors and actresses of the time, from actor-managers like Sir John Martin-Harvey and Sir Frank Benson, to popular artistes like Gertie Millar and Lily Elsie. From opera houses to music halls, he absorbed a huge range of acting styles and cultural experiences that were an ideal introduction to, and education in, the world of the theatre.

His own appearance on stage was delayed for several years by Mam. Learning from her husband's attempt to sabotage Ivor's scholarship at Magdalen, she intercepted a letter from Daly's Theatre, to which Ivor had applied for a role as a chorus boy. She wanted him to be a great composer; he had already had work published and performed, and clearly had an ear for a good tune, so why throw away a dignified and lucrative career for the dubious benefits of a bit part in musical theatre? Her son should be conducting a chorus, not joining one.

It took some time for Ivor to realise what had happened. At first he thought there was a delay in the theatre replying. Eventually he decided to ask them directly, only to hear that he had been invited to an audition but, as he had failed to turn up, he had lost the chance of a part. Furious, he confronted his mother in a classic teenage vs parent row that was all the louder and more hysterical because of the intense, and somewhat self-consciously theatrical relationship between them.

There was a consolation for him, in that he had persuaded her to move apartment, so from 1913, when he was twenty, Ivor lived, with Mam (with David still an occasional, pipe-smoking, character on the family stage) in a flat above the Strand Theatre. This was ideal for two purposes – it was above one theatre, opposite another (the Gaiety) and within walking distance of a dozen others. It was also, and this was crucial for keeping up Ivor's tan – the possessor of a sun terrace, an area of roof that looked down over the Aldwych (the Waldorf Hotel was next door) and across the Thames. It was the perfect base for Ivor.

Ivor at home, 1920s

Having spent the winter in the flat, as it was later, and simply, known to all theatrical London, Mam decided that what was needed was some fresh air, and in the summer of 1914 she took her singing pupils to a campsite at Biggin Hill. Ivor hired a gypsy caravan, the *Tatler* sent a photographer to record the rustic charm, the pretty girls in long dresses, the florid and formidable Mrs Novello Davies and her floppy-haired, alluring son. The piece was an instant success, and gave welcome publicity to mother and son's careers, but the Bohemian idyll was cut short by the outbreak of the First World War.

Ivor, c 1920

THE FIRST WORLD WAR

Biggin Hill may have seemed safer than London, but when Zeppelins were sighted in the countryside, Mam decided that if she was going to be bombed she would rather have her creature comforts around her, so they relocated back to the Aldwych.

The nation was in the grip of patriotic fervour. In what seems, with the benefit of hindsight and a radically different culture, an astonishing move, tens of thousands of young men volunteered to join the armed services, eager to fight for King and Empire, and determined to win some glory before the war was over. Everyone was convinced that it would be a short war – everyone except Field Marshal Lord Kitchener, who knew it would be a prolonged and bloody conflict, and who met his own early death when the battleship on which he was travelling to Imperial Russia was sunk, creating one of the many intriguing 'if's of history – what if he had reached Russia, and made a radical difference to the war on the Eastern Front? Could he have averted the Russian Revolution?

The nearest that Ivor had come to Russian politics was seeing, like most of the theatre-going class of Edwardian London, the Ballets Russes. Another strikingly good-looking young man (though older than Ivor) who was dazzled by the colour and the choreography that Diaghilev brought from St Petersburg to London, was Rupert Brooke, the poet whose *The Soldier* – 'If I should die, think only this of me, that there's some corner of a foreign field that is forever England...' – was to be an elegy for a lost generation. Brooke's poetry was promoted by Eddie (later Sir Edward) Marsh, a highly educated man of private means, who had a penchant for beautiful young men.

After he lost Rupert Brooke to a mosquito bite and the resultant septicaemia en route to the Dardanelles, Marsh desperately needed someone else to love and help, and when he was introduced to Ivor at the theatre during the War, their shared admiration for Lily Elsie (the first Merry Widow on the London stage) as well as Ivor's looks and Marsh's charm (and ability to open the right cultural and social doors) drew them together in a friendship that was to last the rest of Ivor's life. It was cruel enough for Marsh to lose Brooke, but when Ivor predeceased him while still at the peak of his creative powers, he lost the will to live.

It was Eddie Marsh who rescued Ivor from quasi-active service and got him a Whitehall job that enabled him to continue living at home, in the flat, rather than in barracks, and to see, and write music for, the various shows that kept public morale going during the four years of War.

Ivor had not volunteered for service, but was eventually conscripted, and chose to enter the Royal Naval Air Service, which had an attractive uniform (which he supplemented with silk scarves of un-regulation cut and colour) and offered the modern and relatively un-messy (God forbid a stay in the trenches) mode of waging war. Despite getting on well with his co-pilots, who included Ben Travers, the writer of the Aldwych farces that amused inter-war England, Ivor proved disastrously inept as a flyer, and was told that, through a series of crashes, he was doing more damage to the Allies than the Luftwaffe.

In fact, his subsequent transfer to non-combatant duties and a war spent composing tunes for West End shows was not simply down to his hopelessness as a pilot, or Eddie Marsh's undoubted ability at pulling strings (though the latter helped), but was a recognition of the fact that he had already, before conscription, provided an enormous public service through writing one of the most popular, and poignant, songs of the First World War, a song that was included in a national newspaper's poll, taken in 1999, of the top 100 songs of the twentieth century.

Inspired by patriotism and a wonderful chance for public acclaim, Mam announced, shortly after she and Ivor returned to the Aldwych from Biggin Hill, that she would write a song to boost the war spirits of the nation's young. When she triumphantly produced the finished work, Ivor was appalled. His reputation would be as badly damaged as hers if this travesty were to be published. There was only one way to dissuade Mam, and that as to produce a hit himself.

Although he had an easy way with tunes, and had one in mind for the war song, he realised that he needed a lyricist. He found a willing helper in Lena Guilbert Ford, an American-born poetess who lived near Mam's old flat in Maida Vale. She came to the flat and sat next to Ivor as he played through the tune. Neither of them were able to come up with the initial inspiration for the subject of the song until, in best Hollywood style, a maid came into the room to stoke up the fire.

"That's it!" cried Ivor, and wrote down the phrase 'Keep the Home Fires Burning'. He also provided most of the chorus, with Lena producing the verses. The song was given the title 'Till the Boys Come Home' – which is still its official name, although almost immediately it became known by the words that conjure up the simplest, and most powerful image of the whole song. Much of the poetry of the rest of the words came from the lyricist, who worked on them at her own home, and telephoned the results through to Ivor – an early indication of how this most apparently sentimental and nostalgic of composers was actually a product of, and took full advantage of the facilities available to, the modern world.

If the maid's energetic stoking of the fire was like a scene from a film, so was the first public performance of the song, which was given at a Sunday League concert at the Alhambra Theatre, Leicester Square. Sybil Vane, a talented Welsh singer and pupil of Mam, included the song in the second half of the concert, and was accompanied at the piano by Ivor, who was fond of recalling the event:

'I remember how intimidated I was when I walked onto the stage and found the band of the Grenadier Guards on a platform at the back. Sybil sang the first verse and the refrain. Then, as she began to repeat the refrain, to my utter astonishment I heard the audience joining in.

When the refrain came after the second verse they came in with us. After that they sang it as if they had known it all their lives. Eventually we had to sing it nine times before they would let us go.'

Ivor was an overnight sensation. Like Lord Byron he awoke

to find himself famous, and swiftly found that he was rich, too. This was prize enough in itself, but was also a sweet revenge against his usual publishers, Boosey's, who had turned down the song. As happened throughout his life, he proved his critics spectacularly wrong, without having to rub their noses in the fact – his public did that for him.

'Keep The Home Fires Burning' became an anthem at the front, and, for obvious reasons, for civilians at home. As the war continued and the casualty lists lengthened, it tended to be played in a slower, more poignant tempo and arrangement, rather than the tub-thumping way it had first appeared, and like that other great patriotic piece, Land of Hope and Glory, it lent itself equally well to both interpretations.

Abroad, it was sometimes mistaken for being the English National Anthem, so often was it played by military bands and by civilian ones welcoming British soldiers at railway stations, ports and depots. When America entered the war in 1917 her troops took the song to their hearts, too. The tune was a rousing one to march to, while the lyrics had an international appeal, unlike those of Tipperary, with references to the unpronounceable 'Leicester Square'.

Ivor's power as a morale booster was harnessed by the Government at the end of the war, when he was sent to Stockholm, capital of neutral Sweden. The Germans, desperate for new allies as their old ones, Austria, began to collapse, had sent classical orchestras to win the hearts of the Swedes for German culture, and their talent for cabaret was appealing to Stockholm's younger set. Ivor seemed the perfect answer – handsome, young and in uniform, of a similar age to his target audience, yet already a highly popular composer.

This popularity rested not just on the success of 'Keep the Home Fires Burning' (a success that was not long shared with Lena Guilbert Ford, who was killed in a Zeppelin raid on London) but on a series of shows for which he had written music during the war. He contributed a song to *The Bing Boys* at the Alhambra, and wrote many of the songs in André Charlot's revue *See-Saw* at the Comedy Theatre in 1916.

That same year he wrote much of the music for *Theodore and*

Ivor and Lily Elsie in The Truth Game, 1928

Co. at the Gaiety Theatre. His work was lucky to see the light of day as Ivor, who had finally produced the score at the last minute, having been unable to work up his creative energy over a longer period, left the music in a taxi, and had to re-write the whole thing from memory inside the theatre – shades of Sheridan being locked in a dressing room until he had finished writing a play.

In 1917 Ivor contributed music to a musical comedy, *Arlette*, at the Shaftesbury Theatre, and also wrote the music for *Tabs* (for which P G Wodehouse was a lyricist) at the Vaudeville, a show produced by André Charlot and starring Beatrice Lillie.

His new-found fame gave him the entree to any society he chose, but rather than social climbing as many other people in his position would, he chose to use it to opens doors in the theatre world and, in particular, to meet his idol, Lily Elsie.

Ironically their meeting took place in the grandest of circumstances – at No.10 Downing Street. Ivor had met the Prime Minister's daughter, Elizabeth Asquith, and persuaded her to invite Lily Elsie to tea, where he would play some of the music from an operetta than he had written. The meeting did not go at all as planned:

'My heart was beating so violently when we were introduced that I loudly hiccuped! This started us both giggling…I played her the music, but she didn't hear it. Outside, on the Horse Guards Parade, the band was blaring away full tilt. That was bad enough. In addition, Mrs Asquith insisted on performing impromptu solo dances to each tune. Much as I adore Lady Oxford [as she became] on that occasion I would have given my soul to see her carried off by a hawk.'

His constant stream of tunes, his youth, his looks and his success with young audiences combined to make him the ideal candidate for the propaganda visit to Stockholm. He was not just a composer of military tunes but of fashionable musical comedies and revues. Swedish women would surely want to mother or marry him. One can almost see his qualifications being ticked off approvingly by a committee of red-tabbed staff officers in Whitehall. As it happened, Ivor's ability to change the course of the war was not tested for long, for after less than two months in Stockholm the Armistice was declared. The war, to all intents and purposes was over. He had survived, had worn the King's uniform, had become, at the age of 21, a rich and famous man. Now aged 25 he was an established part of the London musical theatre, with a stylish flat in the centre of town, above one theatre and within walking distance of several more.

His struggle to get onto a stage rather than write for it, was to be frustrated for a further three years, however, for, unbeknown to him as he celebrated in Stockholm on Armistice Night, his dream of becoming a famous actor was to be realised, not on stage, but on screen. Ivor was about to become a movie star.

Ivor, 1920s

FIRST FILM & THE EARLY 20s

Ivor's first reaction to Peace was to get out of uniform, back to the theatre, and to have some fun. Royalties from 'Keep the Home Fires Burning' – or 'Keep the HFB' as he called it – had enabled him to hire a country house for week-ends during the War, and meant he could afford to travel wherever he wanted. Remembering the fun he had had in 1912, and inspired by Mam's accounts of her experiences during the War, he decided to go to New York.

Mam's excursions to New York make interesting reading, and are a reminder that, until the late 1920s, she was still an internationally known figure in the music world. Ignoring the threat from U Boats she had insisted on living and teaching in New York for months at a time during the First World War.

During the 1920s she continued this pattern, regardless of her son and husband's increasing concern at her being abroad for such long periods:

'I did not think it wise to tell my immediate family of my intention to teach in New York, or they might have objected to the prolonged stay that this would entail, so I took just enough money along for a short stay there, not to excite any suspicion.'

While in New York she met, separately, two Broadway stars who were to become leading ladies in her son's musicals: Dorothy Dickson (who, with her husband Carl Hyson, was originally known as a dancer rather than a singer) and Mary Ellis.

While in New York Mam enjoyed life to the full, and shocked polite society with her contemptuous refusal to observe a colour bar among her friends. As usual, she displayed a Napoleonic daring in her reaction to the norm, deciding not only to entertain blacks at home, but to do it with as much publicity as possible:

'It is now the fashion of those who have had a surfeit of the usual night-clubs to invade Harlem for entertainment, but in the days of which I speak there was no such 'fraternising', and when I held a big reception and dance for coloured guests only, great was the consternation of my friends, especially one pupil in the best social circles, who hailed from the South. She thought I had gone quite crazy!'

In due course, the combination of changing fashions, old age and the Wall Street Crash were to bring Mam's American sojourns to an end. Once the money had finally run out and Ivor had ordered appropriate action taken, even she had to concede that she had met her Waterloo:

'I suddenly gave way…especially when I found that a firm of attorneys had been approached to wind up my affairs in New York and relieve me of all responsibility.'

This, however, was well in the future when Ivor sailed for the States. With him went his partner, Bobbie Andrews, a young actor whom he had been introduced to during the war. They met, appropriately, in a theatre. Bobbie was an actor of some years experience, so they had a lot in common, and after the initial excitement their affair settled into a lifelong partnership that was clearly of value to both of them.

On the face of it, Bobbie got by far the best side of the bargain. Not only was his partner one of the best looking young men in London, he was a household name when they met, and shortly after that went on to become a massively popular film, stage and musical star.

Not only did he provide Bobbie with companionship (Ivor soon turned to others to liven up his sex life, and Bobbie had his own sideways flings) he gave him a place, centre stage, in a domestic life that was a constant round of parties, dinners and night-clubs (one of which, the Fifty-Fifty, in Soho, Ivor co-owned in the 1920s), surrounded by glamorous and talented people of both sexes.

In addition to a private role, Ivor also cast Bobbie (and his sister Maidie) in several of his plays, and they were together both on stage and at home during the run of *King's Rhapsody* when Ivor died, in March 1951. This was half a lifetime away when they sailed for New York, however, and their time there was carefree, fun and with all the speed and excitement that New York had to offer. Ivor's reputation as a nostalgic dreamer with his face set against the modern world was given the lie time and again by his thirst for the new and the exciting, and his fascination with the best that America had to offer.

Among the people that Ivor was to meet in a blitz of parties that required a constant trans-Atlantic transfer of funds from his London bank account, was Constance Collier. A dark, almost swarthy, actress, she had made her name in New York as well as London, and was to become one of his closest friends and the co-author of his first stage play to win over the critics as well as the audience.

On the return crossing from the States, in the autumn of 1919, Ivor received a message from his London agency. Louis Mercanton, a French film director, was looking for a young man to play the lead in a film about love, betrayal and murder, set in Sicily.

Mercanton had not been impressed with the pallid row of actors' photographs, but had seen a photograph of Ivor that Ivor had sent to Rudolph Meyer of the Daniel Mayer Company. Mercanton thought Ivor's dark good looks were ideal, and asked for him. The agency explained that he had no acting experience (they were too tactful to use the word 'talent') and that he was making a very good living as a composer, but Mercanton persisted. Surely, as they represented the young man, and as he was proposing to cast him in the lead of a major movie, they would at least ask him?

When Ivor received the request he was delighted but undecided. Bobbie, no doubt with visions of film premieres in addition to the current round of theatrical first nights, pressed him to accept. The film, called *L'Appel Du Sang* on the continent, and *The Call of the Blood* in Britain and the United States, was great fun to make, not least because it was shot on location in Italy, so Ivor got a prolonged dose of sun – as well as a poisoned foot when he injured it on the rocky coastal paths where a lot of the action takes place, and where his character is killed.

Ivor's co-star was Phyllis Neilson-Terry, the daughter of the golden couple of Edwardian theatre, Fred Terry (brother of Ellen, and uncle of John Gielgud) and his wife, Julia Neilson. A tall, rangy girl, she played his wife in *The Call of the Blood* and, in real life was to become one of his many close women friends. Ivor's sexuality never precluded friendships with women, and with some of them the friendship was of a definitely romantic nature, but any attempts at a physical realisation of these attachments proved unsatisfactory, a phenomenon that is treated with great skill and a straightforward delicacy in Rhys Davies' novel, *The Painted King* (Heinemann, 1954) a thinly disguised description of Ivor and his career.

None of these entanglements were allowed to get in the way of his sex life, which was pursued actively and frequently when he was younger, and resolutely in his later years. He seemed to prefer nice young men rather than the more dangerous, in every sense, rough trade that some of his fellow thespians enjoyed, and for obvious reasons he found it more convenient, and interesting, to have affairs with young actors. One such relationship, with Christopher Hassall, was to develop into a highly effective writing partnership that produced six musicals.

Ivor's reputation for being able to seduce anyone he chose was given an amusingly apocryphal status in relation to Winston Churchill. Ivor, it was widely said, was the only male with whom the Great Man had (in Ivor's youth and Churchill's middle age) been tempted to have sex. Asked at a dinner party whether the rumour was true, and what – if it was – it had been like, Churchill is said to have puffed meditatively on his cigar and replied, with a smile, "Musical!" 'Musical' was a contemporary euphemism for gay, which makes it an even better story.

Whatever the truth about his one-night stand with Winston, it is certainly the case that Clementine Churchill had an almost morbid fascination with Ivor. She was present, according to the *Daily Sketch*, at a premiere of *The Call of the Blood*, along with other society luminaries like Lady Howard de Walden and Lady Diana Cooper. Her evident admiration for Ivor and his career extended to standing among the enormous crowds that lined the route to Golders Green crematorium with Ivor's other fans for a glimpse of his coffin. It would be fun to imagine that this interest stemmed from her wondering how this man had managed, albeit only once, to tempt her husband from the straight and narrow, but the real explanation is, as ever, probably the simplest – that she,

Ivor, 1920s

like millions of women of all classes, found him irresistible.

Women were to make up the majority of his fans, as well as a majority of his friends. Those who knew him were well aware of his relations with men but though this prevented consummation it did not preclude conversation or his infectiously enjoyable company. Those who did not know him personally, ie the vast majority of his fans, were unaware of his being gay for a number of reasons.

First was the simple fact that homosexuality was not mentioned in the 1920s in the way that it is now. As well as being socially unacceptable, it was, of course, illegal. For men. Women were saved from the nation's jails because Queen Victoria, on being asked to sign the appropriate Bill making homosexual relations illegal, refused to believe that women would engage in such behaviour.

Her grandson, George V, who was an admirer of Ivor's music, thought that "men like that shot themselves." Anyone who met Ivor would swiftly have realised that he was a "man like that" but perhaps the King-Emperor made allowances for the fact that Ivor was in theatre.

The second reason for Ivor's private life being unknown was the vastly less intrusive press of those days. Open secrets in Society circles were kept very much to those circles, the most dramatic example being the affair between the Prince of Wales and Mrs Simpson during the mid 1930s, which only hit the headlines when it had developed into an unstoppable Constitutional crisis.

The third reason was that Ivor was surrounded – in private as well as public life – by a galaxy of female beauty, from Edwardian pin-ups like Gladys Cooper and Phyllis Dare to sleekly lovely divas like Mary Ellis and home-grown beauties like Roma Beaumont and Vanessa Lee – not to mention international stars including Greta Garbo and Linda Christian. His genuine pleasure in their company was plain to see in every press photograph or newsreel clip, and his female fans drew the obvious, and wrong, conclusion.

In a sense, however, the conclusion was only partly wrong. The late 20th century's obsession with sex overlooks the fact that, important though it may be, it rapidly ceases to the primary cement in many – if not most – relationships, being replaced more by a sense of companionship and affection. In the 1920s the sexual revolution (despite the best efforts of Marie Stopes) was a long way off, however hedonistic the tiny group of Bright Young Things immortalised in Evelyn Waugh's novels may have been.

Ivor may not have been sexually compatible with women, but

he was not just fond of them, he was romantically attached to a number of them in the course of his life, and his temporary infatuations, and lasting friendship, were as fervent and as emotionally sincere as a heterosexual man's. An example of this characteristically romantic impulsiveness was when he first saw, and was swept away by, Isadora Duncan, in 1923, when she was well past her prime:

'I saw Isadora Duncan dance at the Prince of Wales Theatre... when she first appeared I was intensely disappointed, and only saw a fat woman with a rather lovely face. "Absurd!" I thought. She shouldn't be allowed to dance. She should remain a legend." But ten minutes afterwards I was at her feet.

The next day I was lunching with a companion at the Savoy, and suddenly saw Isadora sitting among a group at a neighbouring table. I dashed to the florist's just outside and bought every rose in the shop – about six dozen! With my arms full of flowers I went across to the Savoy and laid them on the table in front of her...She told me she was going to Russia in four day's time. During those four days I don't think we were apart for more than four hours! I never saw her again.'

The fourth and final reason was wish fulfilment. Here, at the start of the 1920s, was a beautiful, highly eligible young man with money, fame, and a fascinating career. As he developed as an actor in the course of the 1920s, and became physically accessible in the sense that he had to arrive at and leave stage doors on his way to and from work, and appeared in public to promote his films, he became the target of thousands of would-be Mrs Novellos, whose desire for him was matched only by their ruthless shouldering-aside of their potential rivals in the scrum to get a sight of, and preferably a hold of, Ivor.

This hysteria, which pre-dated the Bobby-Soxer fans of Sinatra and the screaming fits associated with Beatlemania, was just as real, and intense. That it happened in the more sedate 1920s is all the more of a tribute to Ivor's personal magnetism, and re-enforces the fact that he was, in every attribute and aspect of fame (other than drug-taking) the first superstar. He may not have had his assistants sew up his flies in the way that Dirk Bogarde was reported to have done for public appearances in the 1950s, but

MacQueen Pope, Ivor's PR manager for many years, records how his clothes were ripped on occasion, and once, when he had been pushed into the safety of a waiting limousine, his fans tore the rear door off!

Those who were unable to travel to theatres where he appeared had to be content with cinema magazines, press cuttings, and a series of cigarette cards, part of a 'Famous Cinema Stars' series, which showed Ivor in a variety of film roles. Most of them show a man looking incredibly camp, but this was both a more innocent age and also one where, in a prelude to social trends and fashion styles later in the century, an androgynous appearance, for both boys and girls, was the height of fashion.

The Call of the Blood, released in 1920, had met with praise from Parisian critics (and from Sarah Bernhardt, who thought him thrilling) and the Sunday Times had concluded that 'The success of the film is really due to Mr Ivor Novello'. Thrilled by reviews like these, Ivor's ego was kept in check by Bobbie Andrews' caustic humour. On reading a review that gushingly praised the cinematography, claiming that 'Mr Mercanton can make even the rocks act' Bobbie announced: "That's nothing! He can even make Ivor act!"

The film deserved praise for its art work, as it is still very easy on the eye, with good location photography. It has a robustly period attitude to national stereotypes, for Ivor's character is, despite his Italian appearance, an Englishman. The trouble is his grandmother was Italian, and this infusion of foreign blood – hence the title of the film – is the reason for his somewhat suspicious friendship with his handsome and 'inseparable' servant, Gaspar, as well as the adulterous affair with an Italian girl that leads to his murder by her father. The speech captions are on attractively decorated panels, though the language is sometimes as romantic as the scenery. One narrative caption states: 'Morn, with rosy hand unbarred the gates of light'.

Ivor's next film, *Miarka* (1920) was also a French one, in which he appeared with the legendary French actress, Réjane. Years later, in an interview, he recalled his pleasure in acting with her, in what was to be her last role:

'She was an old lady with great burning eyes and a devastating smile. There was a death scene in the film; her acting in this was marvellous; possibly she had a presentiment, for she said to me: "This is just a dress rehearsal." I wonder, did she know? She died two weeks after the film was finished.' She came close to making a less timely, and dignified, departure from this world, during some location filming at a church, which was sacred to French gypsies.

The romantic gypsy motif, which he had toyed with at Biggin Hill, and was to be a recurring theme in his films and musicals, made a first appearance in this one, whose plot made his later, Ruritanian, confections seem straightforward.

The girl in the title role of *Miarka* was Desdemona Mazza, who had played his illicit love interest in *The Call of the Blood*, and they were directed, again, by Louis Mercanton. The heroine, engaged to a gypsy prince, falls in love with the adopted son of the local gentry (Ivor) who turns out to be, in reality, a gypsy prince himself.

This use of a gypsy theme nearly backfired violently, as Ivor remembered:

'The scene of the story was partly laid at Les Saintes Maries, in the Rhone Delta, where, according to the legend, the Three Maries and their gypsy handmaid Sarah landed from their voyage across the Mediterranean…and where for centuries the gypsies of all Europe have congregated on an annual pilgrimage in June.

'The camera was clicking like mad, Réjane acting like an angel, I dissolved in tears by her bedside, when suddenly a menacing crowd of gypsies broke in upon us. In their eyes the cinema was an invention of the devil, and our proceedings a sacrilege…It was an uneasy moment. The men of our party made a circle round Réjane, who showed no sign of fear, and carried her up the steps, through the church and at last, to our great relief, safely into the open…we retreated with what grace we could back to the chateau, where with much ingenuity Mercanton rigged up a crypt in the great barn.'

The film served its purpose in that it gave his cinematic career a forward momentum, but it was far from distinguished as a work of art, and the lack of enthusiasm for this second coupling of the two stars was reflected in the review given it by a cinema magazine, the *Bioscope*, which gave star billing to a circus bear, for whose performance, it claimed, 'no praise can be too high.'

Ivor's next film, Carnival, came out in 1921 and, apart from showing his increasingly famous profile to full advantage, has little to recommend it to film historians. By contrast, *The Bohemian Girl*, also made in 1922, is highly watchable, with excellent performances from Ivor and his co-star, Gladys Cooper, who was to be an important stage and screen partner, a friend, and a rumoured fiancée. She was convinced that she could 'cure' Ivor, but this was not to be. She did not know that in 1923, and she was as keen as any of his fans on getting to know Ivor better.

From a theatre – and film – historian's point of view, the most interesting feature of the movie (apart from the improbable sight of C Aubrey Smith as a gypsy leader) is the appearance, in a cameo role, of the great Ellen Terry. She was the most beautiful as well as the most talented actress of the Victorian age: we have her first husband, G F Watts' paintings as well as contemporary photographs as proof of her looks, and the records of critics and theatregoers during her long partnership with Sir Henry Irving as testament to her talent. By 1923, however, she was a distinguished, but old and rather forgetful lady.

Looking uncannily like Queen Elizabeth, the Queen Mother was to in her later years, Ellen Terry conveys an other-worldly quality in her role as a nurse – a less bawdy version of the one in *Romeo and Juliet*. To see the doyenne of the 19th century stage in a silent movie made in the third decade of the twentieth century is an extraordinary experience.

Also in the film was Constance Collier, playing the Queen of the gypsies. Her friendship with Ivor was renewed by their filming together, and by his great kindness to her after her husband's sudden death. A remarkable actress in her own right, she was already overshadowed by a new generation, and the reviews (which were mixed) of the film largely concentrated on the novelty value of seeing Ellen Terry on screen, and on the performances of the two leads. *Picture Show* concluded that Ivor had 'every quality under the sun to make a screen star', and by now movie makers were in agreement.

Today's viewers would pick up on some of the unintentionally funny aspects of the film, such as the highly unconvincing fight

Ivor in D W Griffith's The White Rose, 1923

between Ivor and a bear, which is clearly a man in a bear suit. One would also ask how many nineteenth century gypsies wore lashings of Brylcream, and, speaking of hair, when the narrative jumps forward twelve years (and the heroine is transformed from a child actress into the dazzling Gladys Cooper), Ivor doesn't look a day older, and the only physical difference is that between the earlier and later takes he had clearly had a session with a less distinguished barber.

Adrian Brunel was sufficiently impressed to cast Ivor in the lead role as *The Man Without Desire* (1923), where he played a Venetian nobleman who, thwarted in love, takes a potion that keeps him in a state of suspended animation for two hundred years. The trouble is that when he is brought to life, his two centuries of lifelessness have taken away his physical ability with women (hence the film's title) and although he has a romance with the descendant (and spitting image, of course) of his original love, he is unable to make a woman of her and, being less than an ideal man, swallows poison. Two endings were shot (the film industry was already bending artistic integrity to commercial interest as deduced through focus groups), in the second of which Ivor and his new lover (played, as was the eighteenth century one, by Nina Vanna) enjoyed a happy ending. As it were.

1923 saw two other Novello releases. *The White Rose* was one of the last flings in the career of D W Griffith, one of the greats of the American silent movie era.

As with his first film, for Louis Mercanton, Ivor landed the role through his looks rather than his acting skills. As he later told the critic Hannen Swaffer, Ivor had 'set up' the informal casting session. Knowing that Griffith would be dining in the Savoy Grill – with Swaffer – Ivor made sure that he had a table in view of Griffith's, that his profile was shown to best advantage during the meal, and acted rather than ate his way through it. Griffith, unaware of this manipulation, was intrigued, and on the strength of his good looks cast him in *The White Rose*.

In it Ivor played a young priest driven into sin by a waitress called Teasie (Mae Marsh). Neither the critics nor the public liked it, on either side of the Atlantic. It was a nail in the coffin of Griffith's reputation, and the other seven films Griffith had promised in Ivor's contract failed to materialise. The *Washington Times* noted Ivor's red silk scarf (a taste left over from his flying days) and spoke approvingly of how he was taller and slimmer than Valentino. Others wrote of him in a more satirical vein, including a fan magazine that referred to 'Three New Sheiks in Beauty War', playing up the exquisite good looks of a number of new male movie stars, of whom Ivor was a leading example.

Hannen Swaffer, who had inadvertently played a crucial role in Ivor appearing in the film, described it in unflattering terms, as a movie in which it rained incessantly and people cried a lot. Not one of Ivor's greatest fans, he was bemused by the fact that Ivor had a large and enthusiastic fan club, and seemed surrounded by hangers-on who were unable to offer any constructive criticism. His own reviews probably over-compensated for this, and Ivor was stung, in a very rare move, to write to him after one theatre review: 'Surely you don't pour away all your milk of human kindness on entering a theatre on a first night?'

If *The White Rose* was a failure, *Bonnie Prince Charlie* was a hit – in the United Kingdom, at least. Playing opposite Gladys Cooper again fanned the flames of the public imagination, and they were expected to announce their engagement at any moment.

One cannot blame the public, or the press. While Ivor was hailed in the American newspapers as 'the handsomest man in England', which he described as 'rot' but clearly enjoyed, Gladys Cooper was an Edwardian beauty whose photo, reproduced in postcard form, had decorated trenches from the Channel to the Alps during the war, and who was about to become not only one of the West End's most popular and stylish actresses, but the only woman apart from Lilian Baylis to manage a major London theatre (the Playhouse, on the Thames Embankment). It would have been a match made in heaven.

The rumours about Ivor and Gladys surfaced at various times in their careers, not least because of the frequency, in the early 1920s, with which they acted together on film and, subsequently, stage. In an interview in the mid 1930s Ivor remembered her arrival in New York, when he was filming *The White Rose*. He had been looking forward to seeing her again, but the day before her arrival he happened to pick up a New York newspaper:

Gladys Cooper in her Edwardian pin-up prime

'The first thing I saw on the front page was a large photograph of Miss Cooper; inset, a very small one of me...Underneath, to my intense horror, was the caption : 'Gladys Cooper crosses the ocean to marry Novello, film actor.' As, at that time, Miss Cooper was still married to Captain Buckmaster, nothing could have been further from our thoughts... I went down to meet the boat.

Instead of being able to welcome Gladys in a natural manner I had to shake hands with her very formally and, at all costs, prevent our being photographed together.'

Despite Ivor's protestations, Gladys did have romantic feelings for him, and there was an electricity between them whenever they acted that both their sets of fans were quick to pick up on. Location shooting on *Bonnie Prince Charlie* temporarily dented this ardour, however. Whatever her romantic intentions at the start of filming, by the end of it Miss Cooper had a distinctly more down to earth view of Ivor, and she was particularly irritated by his playing up to his fans between takes and after the end of the day's shooting. A woman who fiercely guarded her privacy off-stage, she didn't care at all for getting close to her fans, and in later life once rebuked her son-in-law, Robert Morley, for inviting a long-standing and devoted fan to tea. "You've ruined her!" she insisted. "She was a perfectly good fan, and now she'll want to be an acquaintance."

Her other pet hate was physical unattractiveness. An otherwise kind and thoughtful person, she saw anything less than beauty as some sort of spiritual failing or character defect, and responded accordingly. Her initial reaction to Robert Morley, who was no-one's idea of Adonis (other, perhaps, than his wife), can be imagined. Ivor, of course, more than lived up to her physical ideals, but in his case he was aware of the popularity it brought and, enjoying being at the centre of an adoring throng, took to mixing with the locals when the film unit was on location. Not only this, but he drew attention to himself by wearing his highland kilt when off duty as well as in front of the cameras, and despite Gladys Cooper's protestations. By the time they had finished filming they were barely on speaking terms.

They overcame this little spat to appear on stage together in August 1923, in *Enter Kiki*, produced by, as well as starring, Miss Cooper. Ivor had made his cherished and long-awaited stage debut two years earlier at the Ambassadors Theatre, on 23 November 1921, in a French play, *Deburau*, written by Sacha Guitry and adapted by Harvey Granville Barker.

Camp, moi? Ivor, early 1920s

EARLY STAGES

Just as the French had given him his first film role so, in a sense, did they give him his stage debut, though the role of 'The Young Man' was far from a starry one. This part may have been a small one, but it was his first one on stage, and he found the experience daunting:

'At rehearsals I quickly discovered the vast difference between acting on a stage and in a studio. When facing a battery of cameras I had acquired complete confidence in myself, but at the first rehearsal of *Deburau* I was overcome with self-consciousness and could only manage to whisper my words. In fact, it was not until the dress rehearsal that I had sufficiently mastered my nerves to be able to articulate clearly.'

Any pre-show nerves were overcome by the friendliness of Madge Titheradge, the female lead, and the fact that Bobbie Andrews also had a part in the play, and he received an excellent notice:

'Ivor Novello...puts into his wooing the respectful ecstasies of 1840. He did very well.'

His second role was as a Chinese youth in a play called *The Yellow Jacket*, which opened at the Kingsway Theatre on 7 March 1922. It had a short run, and was not helped by the fact that Ivor's character rejoiced in the name Wu Hoo Git. The reviewers picked up on his looks more than his acting ability, but while admiring his beauty they could not, like their trans-Atlantic cousins, help noticing that his brand of sexuality was a far cry from the robust virility of Bulldog Drummond, Richard Hannay and other examples of English manhood.

The *Daily Sketch* dryly reported that: 'Ivor Novello scarcely justifies the villain's accusations of "vulgar manliness"' while The Sunday Times thought he 'occasionally lost the heroic in the effeminate'. The *Sunday Times* also referred to Ivor as 'a frank and good-looking youth' – despite the fact that he was now pushing thirty. Throughout his adult life he continued to look far younger than he was, only beginning to show his age towards the end, when he had illness as well as the passing years to contend with. He was able to play a seventeen year old schoolboy on stage and – slightly less convincingly – on film when in his early thirties (in *Downhill*). For a matinee idol this was, of course, an enormous professional advantage, and which he used to the hilt. One has to take his later protestations, which mirrored those of generations of actresses, of boredom with his beauty and desire to be taken seriously as a performer rather than a clotheshorse, with a large pinch of salt.

In the very early 1920s, when he was in his late twenties, he was only able to start a stage career, with no training, because of his youthful looks. That he was able, eventually, to develop into an accomplished, if limited, actor, was a remarkable achievement, but he was able to learn his craft and roll with the critical punches because of his profile.

Ivor might have been expected to return to composing, which he had never given up, despite the effort involved in launching a film career and his first attempts at a stage one, but he decided to press on with his theatrical ambitions, though he continued to compose for the theatre while trying to make a break-through as an actor.

In September 1919 *Who's Hooper?* opened at the Adelphi Theatre in the Strand, where Ivor's *The Dancing Years* was to have an almost permanent home during the Second World War. Based on a play, *In Chancery*, by Arthur Wing Pinero, *Who's Hooper?* featured music by Ivor and by Howard Talbot. Among Ivor's numbers were the typically Novello-sounding 'The Garden of My Dreams' and 'There's an Angel Watching Over Me', but, more interestingly, 'Wedding Jazz', a sign of Ivor's willingness to use the new form of music he had been introduced to in New York.

In 1920 he provided some of the music for *A Southern Maid*, which opened at Daly's Theatre on 15 May, and in 1921 he wrote the music for *The Golden Moth*, which had its first night at the Adelphi on 5 October. P G Wodehouse wrote most of the lyrics for Ivor's numbers, which included 'My Girl', 'If Ever I Lost You' and the rather Bertie Woosterish 'Give Me a Thought Now and Then.'

Ivor also wrote a song, 'Dusky Nipper', with words by his old flying comrade, Ben Travers, for Binnie Hale to sing in *Dippers* at the Criterion in 1922, but his best work at this period was probably for Andre Charlot's revue *A-Z* at the Prince of Wales Theatre, opening on 21 October 1921. The show made the career of Jack Buchanan, an elegant ladies man whose languid style perfectly complemented, and compared well with, the far more nervy and energetic style of Fred Astaire in Buchanan's last big film, *Band Wagon* (1953). At the time *A-Z* opened, Buchanan was still a young man, and he gave the definitive rendition (which he later recorded) of Ivor's 'And Her Mother Came Too.' The song has a very 1920s feel to it, and shows that Ivor could write in comic, as well as romantic, mode. The point was proved by another number in the same show, 'Rough Stuff', in which a woman sings wistfully of how she enjoys being thrown about by the men in her life. Other women might want to be seduced by matinee idols like Owen Nares – Ivor's singer wanted him to throw her down stairs!

However versatile he may have been, his public seemed to prefer sentiment over swagger, and Mam later remembered an Atlantic crossing on a liner in the 1920s, when the then Prince of Wales was a passenger. He was a fan of one of Ivor's revue songs, the 'Land of Might Have Been', and when she conducted the ship's orchestra at a concert, he led the singing. Given the lyrics, time lent the memory a terrible poignancy:

'We shall never find the lovely Land of Might Have Been
You shall never be my King or I shall be your Queen
Days may pass and years may pass and Seas may be between
We shall never find the Land of Might Have Been.'

Ivor resisting Gladys Cooper's charms, Enter Kiki, 1923

Just as his romantic songs were to be his most popular, so it was with stage and film roles, and it was in a romantic role that he made his next attempt at West End stardom. After *The Yellow Jacket* folded, he returned to the Kingsway Theatre on 21 June of the same year, in another French play, *Spanish Lovers*. The *New Statesman* approved of Ivor's 'pathos and languishing grace' in the role of the doomed poet, Javier. The *Sunday Times* rose above its habitual carping, and applauded Ivor's 'big step upward as an actor'.

It was during the run of *Spanish Lovers* that he first noticed how popular he was with the general public, a phenomenon that continued throughout his life, and which will touched on at various points in this book. He recalled how he became aware of the numbers of people waiting outside the stage door:

'As I had done this myself for years, I was not greatly surprised, but I was when I discovered that it was for me they were waiting. Mostly at the beginning it was older women who, as I came out of the stage door, pressed chest comforters on me, believing that the hacking cough which I had to put on for my part really belonged to me permanently...

People began to open autograph books before me. They would say "Are you the Mr Novello who also writes music?" and when I shame-facedly admitted that it was so, ask me for my signature.'

With these performances under his belt, when he appeared at the Playhouse in *Enter Kiki*, Gladys Cooper had good cause to hope for a profitable run, but she was to be disappointed. Disappointment seems to have been associated with every aspect of the production, for even the young John Gielgud, summoned to the Playhouse to audition as understudy for Ivor's part (as he reminded Sir David Frost in a televised interview on the stage of the Playhouse in 1992), watched the show from the front of house for a few evenings before being dismissed.

Ivor thought he was particularly miscast: 'looking, as all my photographs of that period rightly show, like a boy of nineteen, I essayed to play the character of a masterful actor-manager of forty-five.' Neither he nor Gladys Cooper got rave reviews, and Ivor was described by the *Daily News* as 'walking through' his part, but the *Weekly Dispatch* found 'an intellectual quality about Mr Novello's acting which gives promise of brilliant development, if he resists the temptation to become a matinee idol.'

The *Dispatch's* critic had sounded a word of warning, but he was several years too late, and in the next year, 1924, Ivor found a winning combination – writing and starring in his own shows, making a fortune and then filming them the following year to pull in cinema audiences who would never go near a theatre. 1924 was the year of *The Rat*.

Ivor looking to the future, mid 1920s

THE MID 1920s

Ivor had taken the failure of *The White Rose* to heart. He wanted to save his film career, and, equally, wanted to show that he could play tougher, more dashing roles than he one he had been landed with by D W Griffith, or those he had taken on in order to start his stage career.

He came up with a film treatment of a story about a young Parisian rogue, or Apache as the gigolos of the loucher French night-clubs were known, particularly when they added a little robbery to their other activities. The treatment was sent to Adrian Brunel, who had directed Ivor in *The Man Without Desire*, but Brunel was, at that stage, the Man without Money, so Ivor's hope of a new film, of which he was the author as well as the star, was dashed. As always, however, this served merely to spur him on. If the cinema couldn't afford him then he would try his latest area of activity, the stage.

He worked, with his friend Constance Collier, on a play script. Eventually they decided they had a good product, and raised the money to put it on. The play was given the then traditional try-out at the Theatre Royal, Brighton. Ivor and Constance used a pseudonym, David L'Estrange, to hide the true authorship of the play. David was, technically, Ivor's first name, and L'Estrange was Miss Collier's married name. If it was a flop they didn't want to hand the critics ammunition against them as writers as well as Ivor as a performer. As has already been mentioned, his earliest attempts as an actor had been in French plays and films, so perhaps it was an element of superstition that had led him to place the action in Paris

– though the English association of Paris with passion was doubtless a part of the equation.

Ivor's character, Pierre, lived in a platonic fashion (much to her regret) with a pretty but girl-next-door type called Odile, played by the wholesome and sweet looking Dorothy Batley. The real object of Pierre's affection turned out to be the older but fascinating Zelie, played by Isabel Jeans – one of the most attractive actresses of the inter-war years. Zelie was the mistress of a corrupt politician, Stetz (a German name being a sure sign of villainous intent) who happened to fall for Odile. Finding Stetz in their flat, pressing his unwanted attentions on Odile, Pierre knifes him to death, then flees. Odile is tried for the murder but in a dramatic courtroom scene all comes good in the end, and the young couple are reunited, with Pierre at last aware of what he has so nearly lost, pledging his undying love.

The play featured plenty of scenes in a night-club, the White Coffin, which gave the British audience a delightfully wicked frisson, and in the Apache dance Ivor proved himself as slinkily sexy a dancer as his near-contemporary and rival, Rudolph Valentino. The dress rehearsal was a disaster, there had been the usual flurry of re-writes, Ivor and Constance Collier (who directed the show as well as co-wrote it) were avoiding each other for fear of wrecking their friendship over squabbles about the staging, and, memorably, during a brief pause in the seemingly interminable dress rehearsal, the musical director (needed for the dance scenes) staggered, blind drunk, into Ivor's dressing room and shouted: "Of all the ***** plays I have ever seen this is the ***** worst!"

As Ivor went on stage on the first night at Brighton, Constance Collier was acting in the West End. Her dual role, and the distance between her two duties, had not made the rehearsals any easier, or done anything to calm her nerves. By the time she arrived in Brighton, on the midnight train, she was in a state of nervous exhaustion. She was met at the station by Morgan, Ivor's chauffeur.

As the enormous Rolls Royce (Ivor always preferred to travel by Rolls) drove towards the Theatre Royal's stage door where Constance was due to attend the first-night celebration – or wake, depending on the early notices – she tentatively asked Morgan

64

how the play had gone. Morgan's face, which she could see in the driver's rear-view mirror, was like a mask of stone. "I'm very much afraid, Madam" – her heart sank – "I'm very much afraid that we have a hit on our hands!" At this he broke into a smile, and Constance realised that their gamble had paid off.

This had been just as well for Ivor, as in addition to his artistic worries he had received, the morning of the first night of *The Rat*, a letter from his bank informing him that he was £70 overdrawn – a large sum for 1924. As he stepped onto the stage he knew that if the play flopped he would be ruined. As he later wrote in a souvenir brochure:

'It was sink or swim! Happily, it was swim. When I heard the cheering after the first act I couldn't believe it, and it was not until the end of the play, when there were thirty-eight curtain calls, that I realised that the miracle had happened.'

Whatever the response of the Brighton audience, the London press (it transferred to the Prince of Wales Theatre on 9 June, 1924) were of two minds about *The Rat*, even though they could not deny that it was a hit. The aptly named London Opinion said that: 'As a work of art, the value of *The Rat* is about ninepence, at a liberal estimate, but as a box-office attraction…it ranks at about £1500 a week.' The Queen, like every other paper and magazine, was aware of the real authors of the piece (the publicists had let it be known once they were sure it was a winner): 'They must have written *The Rat* with tongue in cheek all the time and they must chuckle a great deal together on the tremendous success of their appeal to the multitude.'

James Agate, one of the century's most distinguished theatre critics, and who was an admirer of Ivor without ever failing to poke affectionate fun at him in his reviews, covered Ivor's first stage success for the *Sunday Times*, and made it clear that he knew who the real author was: 'This play should have a long run. It is a collector's piece, complete in every detail. No cliché in the way of phrase has been omitted and no tag of sentiment neglected. David L'Estrange may possess his soul in peace: the home fires will be kept burning throughout the summer.' The *Sketch* thought Ivor was 'extremely successful in his interpretation of the part of the Apache 'hero' of the piece, and, naturally, he looks very picturesque'

Ivor (left) in front of the mural at the Fifty-Fifty Club, 1920s

while Tatler, which had followed his career with interest since his gypsy days at Biggin Hill, thought his stage presence 'must surely delight even his staunchest admirers. Both in his lighter, more devil-may-care moods, and in his scenes of passion and despair, he is wonderfully effective and affecting.'

Ivor and Constance capitalised on the success of *The Rat's* dance routine in The White Coffin night-club (a scene that was cribbed from Valentino's turn on the dance floor in *The Four Horsemen of*

the *Apocalypse*) by opening a real-life night-club, as the *Evening News*, which used to be a major London paper and rival of the better-known *Evening Standard*, recorded:

'The Fifty-Fifty Club is now being formed in the West End and it is hoped to open it, in its premises in the neighbourhood of Wardour Street, about 1 October. It will be a club primarily for theatrical people, where they will be able to go before and after the shows, and where they will be able to dance, sip cocktails, dine or sup at a reasonable rate. "The Club is to be so called", said

Ivor Novello, one of the prime movers in the venture, because one will get out as much of it as one gives"...The first three hundred members will be exclusively stage folk. The decorations, which will be most striking, will be done by Nerman, whose work in clubs in Stockholm greatly impressed Novello.'

In due course, once the Fifty-Fifty opened, Ivor took far too much out of the club, regularly entertaining large groups of theatre and film stars, their lovers and friends 'on the house.' More damaging was the almost inevitable intrusion of London 'Society', the younger members of whom were rapidly becoming acclimatised to the new fashion for night-clubs, and who wanted to be able to mingle with Ivor and his friends. Eventually the actors for whom Ivor had designed the place were forced out by the numbers of wealthy young members of the public; the rise in prices forced out the poorer actors, the presence of the general public deterred the richer and more famous ones, and the club finally folded.

A more satisfying return on the initial success of *The Rat* was the film version (1925) directed – and adapted for the screen – by Graham Cutts, who was also to direct *The Triumph of The Rat* (1926) and *The Return of the Rat* in 1928. Isabel Jeans reprised her role as the man-eating courtesan, Zelie, and Ivor, of course, starred, along with, in the *Triumph of The Rat*, the delicious Nina Vanna. The film was the first of Ivor's commercial successes in the cinema and contemporary film magazines described it as proving that he was now 'surely one of the world's supreme young men of the screen' (*Kine Weekly*), and the same magazine breathed a (temporary) sigh of relief that 'his bearing and looks are free from any effeminacy.' *Picturegoer* thought that 'Here at last he has found something that really suits him'.

Ivor's pattern of writing and starring in a play, then appearing in the lead role in the film version the following year meant that he was working almost round the clock for the decade from 1925 to 1935, when he finally abandoned cinema (*Autumn Crocus*, in 1934 was his last film) and began writing the series of musicals for which he is primarily remembered today. The early 1920s have already been covered, and in 1924, the year of *The Rat*, he wrote all the music for a revue called *Puppets* which Charlot presented at the Vaudeville Theatre on 2 January. This

Film poster for The Triumph of the Rat, 1926

contained two jazz-age numbers, 'Raggedy Doll' and 'Old Acquaintance Blues'

Later the same year Ivor wrote some of the numbers that appeared in a musical play, *Our Nell*, about the Restoration actress and courtesan, Nell Gwynne. Nell was a subject of perennial interest to the British, not least because her story involved the stage and royalty, two heady ingredients, but primarily because she was famous for her sexual powers yet seemed reassuringly saucy rather than sleazy. She was played, a decade later and in a film version, by the young Anna Neagle, who looks far raunchier than in her later incarnations as a romantic dancer being whisked around Mayfair ballrooms by Michael Wilding, but even in that film there was a sense of innate decency about the character, whatever the state of her morals.

An entirely unexpected by-product of the show, as Ivor discovered, to his horror, was that 'Our England' was adopted as an anthem by Oswald Mosley's Blackshirts when they came to want a decent patriotic song of their own. In due course Ivor's number was overshadowed by the more militaristic tunes coming out of Hitler's Germany, so he was never tarred with the reputation of being Mosley's songster, but it was a close run thing. Ivor's attitude to Fascism will be discussed in relation to the late 1930s and the writing of *The Dancing Years*, but this is a convenient time to mention that, until the onset of the Second World War, he was unconcerned with politics.

This was, in the 1920s, a typical reaction – the war was over, he had survived, he wanted to have fun – but whatever the decade his interests, though wide, were cultural rather than political. He was interested in current affairs only in as much as they related to friends of his or provided good material for plots for his plays, films and musicals. Most of his friends felt the same way, but his insistence on seeing things through theatrical eyes could exasperate them – Noël Coward once hit him over the head with a newspaper when, watching newsreel footage of a Nazi rally in a cinema together, Ivor had commented, in a delighted tone, on how dashing the Fascist uniforms were.

Fortunately none of his other songs led him into contact – however indirectly – with the rougher elements of inter-war politics. In 1924 he published 'The Rat Dance', music to which he had danced in the White Coffin night-club at the Prince of Wales Theatre that year, and in 1925 he produced three songs, of which the best was 'First Up', for *Still Dancing* at the London Pavilion, a comic number about a poor family in which the first girl to get up in the morning tended to be the best dressed, as the sisters had to share a small pool of clothes. This song, like

'Rough Stuff' in *A-Z*, seems politically incorrect today, but raised smiles rather than eyebrows among Ivor's audiences.

The last major show that Ivor contributed to before writing his Drury Lane musicals was *The House That Jack Built*, a revue starring he husband and wife team of Jack Hulbert and Cicely Courtneidge that opened at the Adelphi on 8 November 1929. The same year saw him write 'Give Me Back my Heart' for his play *Symphony in Two Flats*. He wrote a handful of songs after this, but all his best work went into songs written specifically for his musicals.

To return to the mid 1920s and his alternating between stage and screen, 1925 saw Ivor in a revival of *Old Heidelberg* (later turned into a musical and filmed as The Student Prince, with music by Sigmund Romberg). The revival was compared unfavourably to the George Alexander production of some quarter of a century earlier (St James's Theatre, 1903), particularly by the Times, which commented that 'Mr Ivor Novello has youth and good looks as the Prince, but somehow lacks the distinction with which Alexander invested the character when he was no longer young.' *The London Magazine* was far more interested in the sexual chemistry between the two stars (Ivor was playing opposite Dorothy Batley, his Odile in *The Rat*) and published an article in which the two hugged, kissed and gazed into each other's eyes under the screaming banner headline 'How We Make Love.'

The failure of *Old Heidelberg* – which, had it been shorter, might have run for longer – was blamed, by Ivor, on the fact that it was too soon after the War to show a sympathetic German on stage. Whatever the reason for the show's closure, he had the consolation of being immediately offered work by Gladys Cooper in a play called *Iris*.

He was replacing another actor in a non-lead role (that had already gone to Henry Ainley, an ageing matinee idol) but the show – which Ivor joined on 7 April – was at his old stamping ground, the Adelphi, and he enjoyed the experience of acting with Gladys again. The public were happy, too, and the prospect of seeing two movie stars who had been rumoured to be lovers in private life as well as on film, acting

Ivor showing the profile that made him a movie star

live together on stage, almost tripled the box office receipts and saved *Iris* from closure.

The following year saw Ivor at Wyndham's Theatre, off Leicester Square (where, 70 years later, Yasmina Reza's Art seemed to take up permanent residence). He appeared as Benvenuto Cellini in Firebrand, on 8 February 1926, but although he certainly had the dark good looks to play a dashing Renaissance Italian, the play bombed. Hannen Swaffer, in a magazine article a few years later, remembered that he had been so sure of the play's poor quality, and of his correspondingly bad notice, that he had invited Ivor and other members of the cast to a 'Farewell Lunch'. The one good thing to come out of the production was that Ivor and Constance Collier, who acted in it together, decided to have another try at writing a play.

On 16 June 1926, still using the pseudonym that had long since ceased to fool anyone, Ivor and Constance's latest offering, *Downhill*, opened at the Queen's Theatre, Shaftesbury Avenue. The play was melodramatic in the worse sense, and lent itself more to the silent movies than to the stage, a fact that was proved when, in 1927, it was filmed under the direction of the young Alfred Hitchcock. The Times picked up on its cinematic potential in an astute piece that predicted its financial success at the same time as sighing over the plot:

'*Downhill* or (if we may suggest an alternative title) From Public School to the Embankment – a drama in nine short but lurid reels...Mr Ivor Novello has all the glitter and emphasis that piece requires...'

The play did better on tour than in town (a frequent occurrence in the theatre world, and not necessarily a reflection on a play's merits) but no one was in any doubt that, despite the feminine charms of Phyllis Monkman, it was Ivor that the public came to see. In an age when theatre critics were sometimes as enjoyable to read as the writers whom they were sent to review, St John Ervine of the *Observer* summed up the essential nature of the play's appeal:

'When Mr Novello washed his legs in the first scene of this play, one heard the sound of indrawn breath coming from the maidens in the pit. Here was a thrilling spectacle to be described with the utmost particularity on the morrow to the unfortunate maidens who had missed it. His knees, his shins, even his thighs, and his dear little wiggly toes! If there were palpitations in the pit, there were sighs of satisfaction in the gallery. Hitherto life had seemed to be full. Could there be anything more delightful than Ivor's profile which he so engagingly and so frequently exhibited?...How could any maiden hope for more? And then – oh delicious! – someone discovered that Ivor had knees, and immediately Mr David L'Estrange sat down and wrote a play so they might be publicly washed at the same time that his profile was exhibited. Not in vain had the maidens stood in queues for hours! At the end of the weary night they saw his toes.'

Maidenly swooning over Ivor had been going on for years and was to continue until the day of his funeral. A girl's magazine at about this time published, among a story of girlish goings-on at a boarding school, a special section called 'We Should Like Ivor Novello For A Brother'. Among the reasons given are: 'He acts on the films and he acts on the stage, so he gives us the chance of seeing him fairly regularly', 'He can play the piano and compose the most exciting songs', 'He always looks on the bright side of life' and, best of all – and completely untrue – 'He would rather smoke a pipe than a cigarette, and all girls really prefer men who chew on pipes.'

This fan worship was not restricted to magazines. The crowds of fans that gathered outside the theatres in which he appeared have already been mentioned. Fans were graded from friends and acquaintances and a lucky few more casual contacts who were allowed into Ivor's always busy dressing room, through the lucky girls who lined the stairs that led to the stage door, down to the general public who clamoured for their hero on the street outside.

It was typical of Ivor that, much as he enjoyed being the centre of this adulation, he never became self-obsessed or vain about it, and was always sufficiently detached to notice individuals in the crowd. It was as a result of this that he came to identify a group of girls, all of them plain and unmarried, who had formed themselves into an unofficial but enthusiastic fan club. Too shy to approach him or push for an autograph, they stood, rocking with a mixture of nerves and excitement, a slight but safe distance from the action. It was their characteristic little movement that earned them their nick-name in Ivor's circle – The Rockers – and when possible he would walk over to them and exchange a few pleasantries with them, knowing the pleasure such a simple act of politeness gave them.

Downhill took up much of 1926, but such was Ivor's constant enjoyment of theatre work, and his desire to continue to improve his techniques through a variety of roles, that he opened in *Liliom* at the Duke of York's Theatre in St Martin's Lane, on

23 December. The play was directed by the influential Russian director, Komisarjevsky, who was an important influence on John Gielgud, but Ivor's chief memory of him was that he had invented a novel smoke effect, which went terribly wrong:

'On the first night…the smoke drifted into the auditorium; the gasping and coughing audience nearly drifted into the street.'

The play was the first step on the ladder to stardom for Charles Laughton, but Ivor, playing the title role, was miscast as a fair-ground barker with violent tendencies. As the *Sunday Times* commented:

'Surely it must be obvious to everyone that this hulking brute must be a brute who hulks and that to present him with the aquiline grace and Latin effrontery of Mr Novello…is to court disaster.'

Hannen Swaffer, who was reviewing the play, was approached by an irate woman. At first fearing that a members of the Ivor Novello Club was going to launch a pre-emptive strike, he was relieved to hear her demand that he write truthfully about how bad Ivor had been; a comment that elicited a spontaneous burst of applause from other theatregoers within earshot of her.

Liliom may have been a disaster but the difficulties that Ivor's theatrical career found itself in were more than compensated for by a huge step forward in his cinema work. With *The Lodger*, he had finally arrived as a movie star, in a vehicle that made the name and reputation of one of the giants of cinema history, Alfred Hitchcock.

Ivor looking pensive in a scene from The Lodger, 1926

ENTER ALFRED HITCHCOCK

Hitchcock's career began in Germany, which was where many of the most innovative film camera and lighting techniques were being developed in the 1920s. The industry was already dominated, in terms of the world market, by Hollywood, but at this stage European cinema was vibrant and self-confident, with no sense of being merely 'art house' or pluckily second division.

Hitchcock's earliest films – *The Pleasure Garden* and *The Mountain Eagle* – were made in Germany, in 1926. He had gone there because at that time German film makers were among the most exciting – and had some of the best camera technology and technicians – in Europe. However, he returned to England to make *The Lodger*, a melodrama based on the novel by Marie Belloc Lowndes. Loosely based on Jack the Ripper, and subtitled 'A story of the London Fog', it opens with inter-cuts between showgirls putting on their make-up and newspaper vendors with placards giving details of the latest victim of a serial killer with a penchant for blonde women.

Known as The Avenger, the assassin leaves a calling card at the scene of every murder. Although there is no actual violence shown to such women on screen, the fact that it is blonde women who are being horribly mutilated off camera is the earliest example of the director's notorious enjoyment of the humiliation of blondes in is later films.

We then find ourselves in a working or lower-middle class household in an unfashionable part of London, near where many of the murders have been committed. The daughter of the household, Daisy (played by an actress known, simply, as June) is an attractive blonde woman. Her parents (played by Marie Ault and Arthur Chesney) have a room to let, to supplement whatever income the father makes – judging from his clothes it isn't much.

In one of the striking visual effects that makes the film such fun to watch now – along with the unintended campery of the theatrical style of acting that silent movies relied on – Ivor arrives at the front door, looming out of the sinister fog, his head covered with a hat, his features swathed in a huge scarf, leaving only his piercing eyes visible to the understandably terrified lady of the house.

Any sensible woman would slam the door in his face, but money is money, so he is taken in and shown the room. The cost of living being considerably cheaper in those days, the speech caption that follows her showing her rooms to the mysterious stranger reads: 'Would two pounds a week be too much, Sir?' On removing his hat, scarf and overcoat, Ivor is revealed as a gorgeous, Italianate young man with a distinctly nervy edge. In one of several clues that hint at his being the serial killer, he immediately turns a painting of a fair-haired young woman to the wall, as the sight disturbs him so much. This, like Ivor's entire demeanour whispers 'suspicious' if not screaming 'guilty', and much of Ivor's over-acting was due to the fact that he had been told to make the audience believe that he might indeed be a mass murderer.

The presence of such an attractive young man excites Daisy, who falls for his looks and his charming, sensitive nature – they share a special moment playing chess in front of the fireside. Unfortunately for Ivor, she has a boyfriend, Joe, a police detective who is working on The Avenger's case. Ivor's strange habit of pacing up and down his room at night (shot from below, with Ivor walking on a glass floor to give the appropriate see-through effect), and his even more worrying habit of slipping out of the house in the dead of night (observed by the landlady, an unbelievably light sleeper with supernaturally acute hearing) sets the parents talking.

Their concerns are passed on to their prospective son-in-law, who has come to have a personal as well as a professional reason to want Ivor dragged away to prison. Having had his suspicions, as well as his jealousy, aroused, he asks his prospective parents-in-law: 'Does this lodger of yours mean any harm to Daisy?' The mother's unintentionally hilarious reply is 'Don't be silly, Joe, he's not that sort. Even if he is a bit queer, he's a gentleman.'

Hitchcock cranks up the tension as to Ivor's motives and potential threat, especially in a scene that was a direct ancestor of the famous shower scene in *Psycho*. Daisy has run herself a bath – we see an overhead shot of her feet in the water, as Ivor quietly approaches the door and takes hold of the handle...After yet another murder has been committed, the detective, with fellow officers, bursts into Ivor's room. After a rough search a revolver and a cuttings file about the murderer's activities are found in a locked cupboard, and Ivor is handcuffed.

In fact Ivor's fascination with the case is due to the fact that his lovely young (blonde) sister was the Avenger's first victim, the pacing about is due to his anguish at her death, and his midnight sorties (and the revolver) are due to his determination to find and kill him.

Daisy, who is convinced of his innocence, manages to create a diversion, enabling Ivor and her to escape. They end up in a pub, where he stands out from the fellow drinkers because, hiding his handcuffed wrists under his overcoat, he cannot take hold of a glass, so Daisy has to lift the glass to his lips for him to take a drink. This curious behaviour draws unwelcome attention to them, so Ivor and Daisy leave. They are swiftly followed by a crowd which forms itself into a lynch mob, and we are treated to a prototype Hitchcock chase sequence. Ivor is quickly run to ground, coming up against railings that guard a drop down to an embankment. He tries to clamber over but is caught by his handcuffed wrists in a quasi crucifixion. On the verge of being beaten to death by the furious crowd, he is saved when a newspaper boy arrives with the news that The Avenger has been arrested. The Christ-like imagery is continued as he is gently handled down from the railings, a scene like that of Christ taken down from the cross.

The film concludes with an epilogue which sees the landlady and her husband welcomed into Ivor's mansion, where he intends to bring Daisy as his bride. Their sycophantic faces speak volumes, and one can almost hear the mother saying "Oh, we knew you was always a good 'un', Sir!" even though she had believed precisely the opposite.

The ending was meant to be reassuring on several levels – the threat to society (The Avenger) has been removed, the gentleman (Ivor) is restored to his proper place – his own, suitably grand, home – and the lower orders are appropriately deferential though, this being 1920s England, the daughter can make the traditional journey from working to upper class through a stage career followed by a good marriage.

Hitchcock wanted the ending to be far more ambivalent, with a lingering suspicion that Ivor might have been The Avenger after all. This would have been more powerful, but was too radical a departure for the film studio, who thought that whatever the suspense during a film, when it ended the public preferred to know exactly where every character stood in relation to the main thrust of the plot.

Hitchcock believed that the studios also thought it would damage Ivor's image to have him cast as a villain, which was another reason why the film had to be rounded off in such a conventional manner. In fact he seems to have had something of a bee in his bonnet about the studio's protectiveness towards Ivor as, years later, he still seemed to resent having to cut an amusing development in a fight scene in the second of the Ivor vehicles which he directed, *Downhill* (1927), on the grounds that it was seen as poking fun at the star.

Whatever the Olympian heights from which he looked back at his earlier work, Hitchcock could have been more gracious in his acknowledgement of Ivor's popularity as a silent movie star, and the boost that these two films gave to the director's career.

The film of *Downhill*, which appeared, like that of *The Rat*, a year after the stage version, is inferior to *The Lodger*, which is why the first tends to be shown frequently at the NFT whereas *Downhill* hardly ever gets an airing. Hitchcock's second English film is not without its finer points, however, particularly in the scenes of Ivor's degradation – the director seems to have as sadistic a relish at seeing a male beauty badly treated as he was later to exhibit with leading ladies.

Ivor's character is a public schoolboy, Roddy, whose best friend, Tim, is sweet on a local shop-girl. The scene where Roddy visits her shop and messes around behind the counter with another

Caricature of Ivor looking like the young Rupert Everett, 1920s

boy demonstrates his comic acting skill. The girl, Mabel, may be going out with Tim but she is more keen on Roddy, whose lack of interest infuriates her. Settling, temporarily, for second best, she gets pregnant by Tim, but, knowing that Roddy's family is richer than his friend's, and hoping to get hold of his body by foul means if fair won't work, she insists on seeing the headmaster. He summons both boys into his study and confronts them with the problem. Tim won't own up and when Mabel accuses him of being the prospective father he is too much of a young gentleman to defend himself at his friend's expense – 'You needn't be afraid. I won't sneak.' After all, he expects to be Captain of School next term, and the school's motto (as the camera reminds us) is 'Honour'. The headmaster summarily expels him, with Ivor being given the unintentionally hilarious line (printed on screen rather than spoken, of course) 'Can I – won't I be able to play for the Old Boys, Sir?'

Those who have never watched a silent movie will assume that having rare snatches of dialogue printed on an otherwise blank screen in between the pictures is incredibly distracting, and disruptive of the flow of the action, but when sitting through a silent film, the word-boards cease to be intrusive, and one almost hears the characters speak them. The pause for the words to appear and be read also seems to give the mind longer to take in the preceding action, and to prepare it for the next – not so much a distraction as a concentration. Single-word frames, like Roddy's father's melodramatic retort to his son's protestations of innocence – "Liar!" – have, in this context, all the more impact.

The movie was more entertaining than the stage play in that Hitchcock was able to open out the action, and perhaps the best scene is set in a seedy night-club in Marseilles. Ivor has ended up here after having run away from home, fallen in love with an actress, inherited a fortune and lost it (thanks to the actress, whose marries him then cleans him out), and descended into the twilight world of dance hosts in the South of France. This last location was a nice touch, as the British public school system has always associated warmth with immorality – hence the cold showers and icy dormitories, combined with a fanatical insistence on boys spending much of their formative years on freezing playing fields.

Hitchcock uses a number of fade-outs in the film, for example from the school playing grounds to Piccadilly Circus, and plays a clever trick on the audience by showing a waiter pocketing what seems to be a purse, but turns out to be a cigarette case – and then pans out to reveal that, in a double trick, the action has taken place in a stage production.

Roddy's degradation is (rather daringly for 1927) fully revealed in a scene, towards the end of the film, which is clearly the work of a master director. The boy, exhausted at the end of an evening of dancing with single ladies, is having eyes made at him by a distinctly unattractive, overweight matron. Despite her weight he responds to her, as she seems genuinely interested in him. As Roddy says, with what proves to be a ghastly irony: 'You seem different somehow...amid all this artificiality'. The woman, realising that his resistance is weakening, goes for the final push; 'Come with me!...You can.' At that moment the night-club proprietor, a woman, opens the heavy curtains to reveal daylight. As the sunshine gradually lights up the room, the camera focuses on the matron's face, and we realise that the heavy make up was to hide not just the ravages of age but...five o'clock shadow! The matron is a man.

Roddy, thoroughly humiliated, runs away to sea, where he nearly dies of a fever. The delirium is effectively caught by Hitchcock, who whirls flashbacks of Ivor's life across the screen, as the young lad thrashes about in his bunk. Eventually, however, the ship reaches London, and Roddy, returning to his family, finds that his innocence has been established in his absence, and his restoration to his proper social position, and to respectability, is confirmed by the final reel, where he not only plays for the Old Boys but scores a try!

Noel Coward at the time of Sirocco

THE COWARD CONNECTION

Ivor met Noël Coward during the First World War. Coward was then a struggling young actor determined to be a star. Ivor was an established name, seven years Coward's senior but a world apart in terms of artistic status and, crucially, financial clout. Both attributes were essential ingredients in the stardom that Coward craved. Ivor's initial impression, however, was anything but glamorous – he was unshaved, tired, and simply dressed in an old overcoat.

Later in the day, when they saw each other again, Ivor was bathed, shaved and in his dinner jacket, looking handsome, relaxed and confident. His transformation provided Coward with a useful lesson in the importance of presentation – at their initial meeting he had thought Ivor looked like an itinerant musician, and at their second he was obviously a part of the West End smart set, yet the two impressions were separated only by a hour of grooming and a decent set of clothes.

Ivor was charming to the young Noël, partly because Noël was a friend of Bobbie Andrews – who, like Noël, had been a child actor – but also because as well as being of a naturally good-tempered disposition (despite the occasional Celtic squalls) he had decided, as a matter of policy, always to be nice to people, whatever their position in life, and regardless of whether or not they were of obvious use to him.

The charm worked on Noël, but with a twist – after Noël watched Ivor and his friends go off to a smart dinner, he returned to his theatrical digs and a sparse supper on a tray, perched on his bed. The contrast between Ivor's life and his rankled, as his memoirs show, and his affection and admiration for Ivor continued to be tempered by a competitive rivalry that both men denied but which clearly existed.

Although Noël and Ivor were, in their prime, both highly successful actors, writer and composers, with professional images and private lifestyles than seemed the epitome of glamour, their talents were quite distinct. Ivor was the better musician, Noël the better playwright. Ivor was, personally, more relaxed and affable than Noël, and had none of the striving for social recognition that characterised Noël's whole life. Which is why Ivor, despite an extraordinary work-load in the late 1920s, never had a nervous breakdown, whereas Noël had several, requiring numerous cruises to recuperate.

In his lifetime, Ivor was more personally popular than Noël, and was more consistently successful – his obituary in the Times noted that:

'As an actor, playwright and composer he occupied a position with the public in general which even Mr Noël Coward, his friend and rival, could scarcely challenge'

Yet since his death it has been Noël's reputation that has survived, not Ivor's. This is partly due to Noël's relative longevity and the fact that , in later life, he was taken to the public's heart in a way that he had not been when younger, but it is also because of the nature of his talent.

Noël was a far more sophisticated playwright than Ivor, and unquestionably wittier, which is why his plays have lasted and Ivor's have not. Ivor didn't have wit, he had humour, which is gentler and sometimes more enjoyable, but depends on particular personalities and circumstances. Humour is also notoriously of its time – jokes that had audiences rolling in the aisles in the 1930s and 1940s (as we know, through recordings) can leave today's audiences cold.

Ivor's humour was a feature of his straight plays and musicals (*King's Rhapsody* occasionally managed wit), but this is largely forgotten today as the plays are never performed – though *Proscenium* and *I Lived With You* would certainly merit reviving – and the musicals are only heard as single songs or in concert versions without the dialogue. Ivor's humour, dependent on personalities and situations rather than deathless prose, can be illustrated by three one-act comedies he wrote for charity performances at the London Palladium.

The Gatecrasher is set in 'A Lady's drawing room in Mayfair', and is peopled by only two characters – 'The Lady' and 'The Lad'. The Lady returns from a party to find an elegant young society burglar in her room. He is surprised to find she is armed: "I never dreamed that someone so attractive could be so blood-thirsty."

She asks why he chose her to rob. He is trying to wriggle out of his predicament, using charm: "Isn't it obvious? I saw you at that ball. I couldn't take my eyes off you." "Really! – but I wasn't the prettiest there."

"No – but you had the best pearls."

She reaches for the phone to summon the police, so he back-tracks.

"You were the prettiest there – by far the prettiest."

"And I had the best pearls?

"And you had the best pearls – the combination was irresistible."

He reveals, after much verbal sparring, that he is not really a burglar, but a would-be lover, who is determined to woo her before she makes the mistake of marrying a man she doesn't love, for the sake of a title and security – his uncle! The final twist in what is a light but engaging plot, that relies on the attractiveness of the actors and the indulgence of an audience who are never quite sure what to believe, is that he turns out to really be a burglar after all, whose fast talking has saved him from arrest. Having convinced her of his innocence before his departure, she grants him a kiss, only to find that he has 'lifted' her pearls during their embrace.

Lady Fandemere's Wynd is less of a gossamer piece, and wittier. It is a pastiche of an Oscar Wilde play, performed by a second-rate touring company, and poking fun at Wilde's endless bon mots and aphorisms. Algy is entertaining friends before they go to the opera:

Algy: Vavasour, I am a gentleman and therefore am the first to give away a lady. Evading the vigilant care of her step-mother,

Lady Eversoe, the fair Rose is joining me here...
Lily: Algy, you are so wicked that you are almost a saint.
Flo: And so the fair Rose is to be awakened for the first time.
Algy: Except by her nurse.
Vavasour: We shall be thinking of you when Siegfried slays the dragon.
Algy: It is Rose that is coming, not her mother.

The person who comes is an old flame of Algy's, whom he has loved and deserted, shortly before she took up a new career in opera – "The moment you left me I developed an enormous soprano voice".

Algy tries to get rid of her, before Rose arrives:

Algy: Out through the window: with the exception of Piccadilly Circus you can reach the opera house by way of the roofs.
Mrs M: And what do I do at Piccadilly Circus?
Algy: A telegraph wire – surely you, an opera singer, can manage a telegraph wire.

The actor then playing Algy announces that the actress playing Rose has been knocked down leaving several pubs on her way to the theatre, so her part is to be played by her mother – a large cockney character with an obsession with bowels and wind. The piece rapidly descends into Carry On Wilde, and with the right cast it would be hilarious.

Love Will Find A Way, subtitled 'A Spectacular Drama in One Scene', lasts 11 pages and involves a pure young governess with the appropriate name of Hazeline Snow, a young aristocrat, a mysterious Polish exile and a 'fast' young French maid, among others.

After we hear the clip clop of hooves, the Butler says: "That's the car now" – a typical Ivor comedy of situation. The aristocrat is dashing and arrogant – his butler refers to him as Lord Ronald – "Don't call me that" he replies, "Just call me Lord." He dismisses "these pure young girls with their eternal crosswords and thick underclothes...I have learned the joys of opium smoking..." We then hear the same clip-clop of a passing horse as he says, of his dissolute lover: "I hear her own private aeroplane landing..."

Ronald's younger brothers don't like the wicked lady: "She comes into our rooms when we are asleep and takes ever so long to say good-night."

Ronald then proposes to Hazeline Snow:

Hazel: Lord Ronald, I am only a governess, but I have my Pride...

Ronald: Show it to me -

Hazel: It's up in my room...

And so on....

All three plays relied for their impact on his presence on stage, and his talent as a light comedian, though they still read well and would lend themselves to being performed at a charity gala today. But even though they are engaging, they are unlikely to be mistaken for Coward's work. It was the difference in style between the two men that made Ivor wary when he was offered the title role in Noël's 1927 play, *Sirocco*.

The story describes the romantic intrigues of a young Italian waiter, and although Ivor certainly looked the part, he thought he would be miscast in the role, which required a more macho roughness than he could provide, particularly in the love scenes which, with their Mediterranean setting and distinctly Latin exuberance, risked seeming overblown at best, risible at worst. His awareness of his deficiency in this area was to be confirmed in a review by the *Sketch*, which sighed: 'Ivor Novello is delightful in his lighter moments, but I wish, I wish he were not always cast for these parts in which he had to be brutal.' Ignoring Ivor's reservations, Noël remained determined to cast him, and finally won the argument by threatening to play the part himself. The idea was so absurd that Ivor, wanting to save the play and his friend's reputation, agreed to appear.

In the event, Ivor's doubts were confirmed at a first night that went down in theatre history as being the definition of a disaster. Although the stalls seemed happy enough, the cheap seats in the gallery took against the play almost immediately – possibly desiring to teach Noël 'a lesson', in the charmless but characteristic English fashion for trying to crush anyone young and consistently

Ivor greets bemused diners in Sirocco, 1927

successful (like Kenneth Branagh in the late 1980s) in order to stop them 'getting above themselves.'

Noël was definitely in this category, and the shouted comments, rumbles and hisses that greeted the play confirmed the fact that he was about to receive what the mob thought was appropriate treatment. Ivor's Latin love-making failed to convince, and the histrionics required of him by the author meant that he would have had little chance in the best of

circumstances, let alone in front of a wildly hostile audience intent on ruining the play.

At one particularly emotional point Ivor had to announce that he was leaving his lover (played, gallantly, by the lovely Frances Doble) in order to go back to his Mamma. A wag in the audience suggested, at the top of his voice, what he ought to do when he got there, and the evening was lost. The curtain call was the most venomously raucous one in West End history. Basil Dean, the director, had sensibly absented himself from the auditorium while the show was on. Returning in time for the curtain, he mistook the uproar for approbation, and had the curtain raised several times on the hapless cast.

Noël Coward, brave and contemptuous in equal measure, insisted on taking the playwright's privilege of joining his actors on stage, and this raised the tempo even higher. He led Frances Doble forward in the teeth of catcalls and abuse, as if the gallery had been cheering her performance rather than assaulting it. The poor woman was in floods of tears, and, in a state of near hysteria, she began to give her pre-prepared curtain call speech. For a stunned moment the audience fell silent to hear what she might have to say. Unnerved by the silence as much as she had been by the noise, she said "Ladies and Gentlemen, this is the happiest night of my life..." before the freshly enraged audience renewed and redoubled their verbal assault.

The difference in the two men's characters came out, as characters tend to do in extreme circumstances. Noël was white with anger, and deliberately infuriated his enemies even more by turning his back on them and congratulating the cast. Ivor, who partly agreed with the critical response to his performance but thought it as ludicrously over the top as some of his lines, saw the funny side of the situation, and started laughing, at which point, mercifully, the curtain was finally brought down. At supper afterwards Noël was still trembling with rage, until Ivor's amused reaction to the whole affair persuaded him to calm down. The show was a byword for disaster for many years, with *Sirocco* entering theatrical slang as a word for a ghastly first night.

This was the last of the stage collaborations between Noël and Ivor, but it did not stop them from working together on two films. In 1928 Ivor starred as Nicky Lancaster in the silent film version of Coward's shocking play *The Vortex*, which had made his name as a West End enfant terrible in 1924. The play described a drug addicted young man whose mother, a society women with a penchant for toy-boys, disgusts him by her refusal to give up her young men and the ridicule to which her current affair is exposing her. Nicky's own shameful secret was homosexuality but, as Coward knew the Lord Chamberlain (a Palace official who continued to censor plays, astonishingly, until 1968) would never allow that particular 'vice' to be presented on stage, he gave him a drug habit instead.

It was the case then (and until very recently) that, despite the Lord Chamberlain, one could treat issues in a more forthright, and morally ambiguous, way on stage than in the cinema. As has already been described, Alfred Hitchcock was frustrated by the need to have *The Lodger* given a happy ending, and blamed that, unfairly, on Ivor rather than the public morality, and studio convention, of the day.

The film of *The Vortex*, however, goes far beyond the normal watering down of the issues raised in a stage play – such as happened in the 1950s, for example, in the Hollywood version of Tenessee Williams' masterpiece, *Cat on a Hot Tin Roof*, where the young husband's essentially gay relationship with his best friend, stated explicitly on stage, was severely diluted into a case of hero worship.

In the film of *The Vortex*, far from being a drug addict, Nicky Lancaster is a prissy young man who dismisses a girl-friend – 'You little rotter!' – when he finds that she is interested in drugs. Worse, his mother is made to state, explicitly, that she does not have a physical relationship with her toy boy – 'You follow me about like a keeper. No wonder people think we are something more than friends…I wish you would stop behaving as though you really did own me, body and soul'.

The production values of the film are distinctly variable, with neighbours simply walking into the Lancaster's house, which is obviously just a collection of painted scenery rather than real walls and furniture. There are some interesting outdoor shots of tennis matches, and Nicky's father, a decent old boy who has never fully recovered from the Great War, comes across sympathetically, but there is a ludicrous caption to Nicky's mother's jealous reaction to seeing her toy boy kissing a girl of his own age – 'You cad! You utter cad!' – and Frances Doble, the ill-fated star of *Sirocco*, vanishes in the jump of a frame in a garden scene.

The whole film is reduced to an emasculated, and utterly pointless pastiche of Coward's exciting and innovative original, and one presumes Ivor only did it for the cheque.

It was entirely for the cheque that he appeared in another film that year, *The Constant Nymph*. This was not a Coward play, but the central role, of Lewis Dodd, a professor who falls in love with an under-age but mature and loving girl (hence the title) had been given to Noël, who played it for a month before undergoing one of his periodic nervous breakdowns and being replaced by a bemused John Gielgud.

Ivor had wanted to play the role himself, and was hurt when he was passed over in favour of the younger (but, at the time, more fashionable) Noël. The constant but unspoken rivalry between them had surfaced again, though Ivor's refusal to take the film role (Gielgud was neither a film name nor a good film actor at this stage) was not just a case of wounded pride at having been passed over for the stage show – he didn't want to rub Noël's face in his later victory.

Michael Balcon was determined to have him, but Ivor was equally adamant that he would not agree, until he came across a country house in Littlewick Green, near Maidenhead, which he instantly fell in love with. Ivor demanded a fee that exactly matched the asking price of the house, and so was able to purchase a country retreat and star in a role he had been keen to play, opposite Mabel Poulton.

The house was re-christened Redroofs, and became the scene of countless week-end house parties until Ivor's death in 1951. The house was long and relatively low, with extensive but manageable gardens, and a simple – indeed rather ugly – but invaluable swimming pool. A set of stone stairs led from Ivor's bedroom down the outside of the house to the lawn, and a garden room where he liked to compose music, and to record his efforts on a large, simple, but at the time technologically advanced recording machine.

Redroofs had a live-in staff, and was where Ivor played host to a large number of stars, but the house was comfortable and the atmosphere both relaxing and fun, rather than luxurious. Unlike Noël he was uninterested in mixing with royalty and the smarter monied classes, preferring to socialise with actors, actresses and directors, people who shared his love and knowledge of the theatre. Cinema was represented as well, and in later years Redroofs was one of the few places where Greta Garbo felt at home on her visits to England.

Seeing her in London was much more difficult, but Ivor found the intrigue great fun – not least because of the inherent theatricality in this world-famous beauty desperately trying to become a recluse – and thereby ensuring an enormous amount of press interest. In the 1940s Gordon Duttson, a young actor and dancer who became his last private secretary, used to send Ivor's Rolls to collect La Garbo from her hotel, hop out of the car before it got there and have it pick up a decoy, while he popped into a taxi and collected her from a back door.

None of this cloak and dagger work had to take place at Redroofs, which was always packed with friends at the weekends. Noël Coward was an occasional visitor, and had Ivor to his country home in return, but both men were, essentially, the centre of their own little courts and kingdoms, and their guests felt more relaxed when there was only one monarch present.

The last word in their battle for fame (and Coward was big enough to report it) came from a stage door keeper – presumably a temporary one, or he would have known to whom he was speaking. He stopped Noël on his way into the theatre where he was performing. "Do you realise who I am?" Noël asked the truculent little man. When he replied in the negative, Noël announced: "I am not only the star of this show, but the author and composer, too!" The door-keeper looked up, removed the hand-rolled cigarette from his lower lip and said, to Coward's mortification: "Right little Ivor Novello, aren't you?"

Ivor and Lilian Braithwaite in the garden at Redroofs, 1930s

THE LATE 1920s

After the fiasco of Noël Coward's *Sirocco*, Ivor needed a success to salvage his reputation. He was aware of his acting limitations, which *Sirocco* had glaringly exposed, but he was equally sure of his strengths, and decided that he should stick to the formula that had worked so well for him a few years earlier – appearing in material written by, and suitable for, himself. Whatever the critics might make of this apparent self-indulgence, he was confident that the public, and therefore the box office, would support him.

Although he was very much a creative artist, his awareness of the importance of finance, which went back to his adolescent astuteness in securing the services of Fred Allen as his accountant, was fundamental to his approach to performing – he did it for fun, but also for the money, and in a typically Ivor way he managed to combine the two, writing the daily box office takings in lipstick on his dressing room mirror. This didn't go down well in later years with Tom Arnold, who produced his musicals, and wasn't happy that his finances were there for all and sundry to see – for the dressing room was invariably crowded with well-wishers, many of whom worked for rival impresarios.

Ivor launched his come-back by writing a comedy, *The Truth Game*. He presented this under a pseudonym, H.E.S. Davidson – which, as David Davies's son, he was. *The Truth Game* opened at the Globe Theatre (now the Gielgud) in Shaftesbury Avenue on 5 October 1928, and was an instant success, which was all the sweeter for Ivor as two of his favourite actresses, Constance Collier and Ellis Jeffreys, had, in turn, accepted the important role of Mrs Brandon, only to pull out on second thoughts. In Constance Collier's case it was because she was convinced that the play was going to be a disaster, and she hoped that her withdrawal would wreck the play but save Ivor's faltering reputation. The only damage this did, however, was to their long and profitable friendship, which took some time to recover.

The role of Mrs Brandon was taken, at the third (and lucky) attempt, by Lilian Braithwaite, who was rewarded for her faith in the play and its author by a series of roles in his other shows. She was already a popular actress, whose commercial clout earned her a large photo in a full page advert in the theatre programme, where she sang the praises, in what the advertisers referred to as 'an emphatic statement', of Pond's Cream:

'I find that little cuts and scratches or irritations of the skin, heal up very quickly after a generous use of this Cold Cream. I use lots of it.'

She was better known, among her colleagues, for her wit than her beauty, and her humour often had an edge to it. Speaking of a rival, she commented: 'She's good, you know, if one can only forget that strange little head on such a tremendous body.' Of an ageing comedienne she said: 'She's learned all the tricks. The trouble is she doesn't know how to perform them.' Perhaps the most silkily savage was: 'I don't think she gave such a bad performance, but the audience was very restless and began to leave before the end of the play.'

This was never a likely event at any play she was in, and *The Truth Game*, being a very 1920s show – light-weight but well constructed and with considerable charm – packed the public in. The central plot is the dilemma that a wealthy widow, Rosine Brown (performed, in her stage comeback, by London's original lead in Lehàr's *The Merry Widow*, Lily Elsie) faces. Rosine is being courted by Max Clement (Ivor) whom she falls for, only to discover that he is a cousin of hers. She had been impressed by the fact that despite a reputation as a lady's man with an eye on the main chance, Max had been keen to marry her, even though in the terms of her late husband's will a remarriage would mean her forfeiting the fortune he had left to her. The twist in the plot is that the next in line for the husband's money turns out to be – Max.

Aided by Mrs Brandon (Lilian Braithwaite), a woman who earns hefty sums of money by providing smart shops with wealthy clients, he manages to restore himself to his rightful place in Rosine's heart, saving her from a rebound (and financially astute) marriage to Sir George Kelvin. *The Times* considered the play to be a curate's egg, denouncing it as 'inane' and 'shallow' before concluding, magnanimously, that it was often 'very good fun'. Theatre World was less critical, focussing on the physical beauty of the lead characters: 'Lily Elsie and Ivor Novello are the most picturesque pair that feminine playgoers could wish to see, and as women form the greater part of any given audience, their complete satisfaction with the entertainment is practically guaranteed in advance'.

This satisfaction was doubly welcome, as the three further films (in addition to *The Constant Nymph*) that he made in 1928 were all disappointing in terms of their box office – though they are of interest to film enthusiasts today.

The Gallant Hussar was one of the last silent movies to be released in Britain, as the public were now demanding talkies. Silent movies were, by 1928, an anachronism, however interesting as an art form, and however beautifully made individual pictures were. They had developed their style in the absence of sound, but the absence had been due to a lack of technology rather than an artistic policy, and now that it was available producers, cinema owners and the public deserted them.

The Gallant Hussar was produced by Gainsborough Pictures, the studio led by C M Woolf and Michael Balcon, which had cashed in on, and helped promote, Ivor's career as a film star. *Film Weekly* thought that Ivor's 'Personal charm as much as acting ability enables him to achieve considerable success' though his personal charms were not helped by an unfortunate moustache which, in one photo on an otherwise splendid publicity poster, makes him look disconcertingly like Adolf Hitler.

The Return of the Rat, which missed the boat, as far as Rat fever was concerned, by a couple of years, was a failure. Ivor recreated his screen partnership with Mabel Poulton, who played a sweet young girl to whom *the Rat* gets married, and with whom he retires from crime into a life of blameless bliss after his previous wife, the older femme fatale of the earlier films, has been murdered and *The Rat* has, after various adventures, handed in the culprit to his old foes, the police.

Having been made as a silent, it had a sound-track hastily added to try to save it, but the effort might as well have been spared. For some reason Herbert Wilcox, the director and, in due course, husband of Anna Neagle, one of Britain's finest (and most under-rated today) screen actresses, decided to film a talking version of *The Rat* in 1937, nearly a decade after the public had shown themselves bored with his Parisian goings-on. Ivor was asked to reprise his role, but sensibly declined, so it was taken by the young Anton Walbrook, who had played Prince Albert to Anna Neagle's Queen Victoria – a role that she was to make her own, not just in *Victoria the Great* (1937) but in *Sixty Glorious Years* (1938).

Finally, Ivor appeared in the last of his silent films, *South Sea Bubble*, in which he played an impoverished descendant of a pirate, who leads a group to a South Sea island in search of hidden treasure, whose discovery leads to a series of conflicts that are only resolved when the treasure is lost at sea. Ivor's moustache made another rare appearance, and although Annette Benson smouldered sexily and Benita Hume looked delightfully pure, the film flopped. The *Bioscope* dismissed Ivor's performance as 'his usual attractive manner of well-bred immobility' while *Film Weekly* thought his 'acting is sometimes quite poor and mechanical,' One of the problems, in Ivor's defence, is that the florid and theatrical mannerisms that worked well in silent films, to which an earlier generation of cinema audiences had been accustomed, had been made obsolete, overnight, by the appearance of talkies.

Once he was in talking films, Ivor was able to adapt to the new medium and give a more relaxed, and convincing, performance. In *South Sea Bubble* he was aware of the fact that, in terms of cinema acting, he was between two stools – unable to emote in the old theatrical style but, without a proper sound track, incapable of giving a 'modern' film performance, so it is unsurprising that he appeared stiff and awkward.

He gratefully returned to the stage the following year with his new play, *Symphony in Two Flats*, which was directed by Raymond Massey and opened at the New Theatre (now the Albery) in St Martin's Lane

Ivor and Benita Hume, South Sea Bubble 1928

on 14 October, 1929. The title, *Symphony in Two Flats*, was a pun on the fact that the action involved two sets of apartment dwellers, one above the other, and that the events on the upper floor – which were tragic, in contrast to the comic relief of the lower level – involved a young composer who enters a music competition.

The composer, David, is married, and poor, and desperately needs to win the first prize. Unfortunately he is also going blind, which places an inevitable strain on his marriage, with the added complication that his best friend is secretly in love with his wife, Lesley. In a misplaced attempt to conceal from him the fact that he has not won, they go so far as pretending that he has – a very short term policy in real life, but this was a 1920s play, so common sense was a minor consideration.

David manages to tune into the radio broadcast of the winning entry, and immediately realises the deception. Appalled at this, he tears off his bandages just at the moment that his friend is comforting the distraught Lesley. Immediately misinterpreting what he has just seen, he throws them both out. His sight is still poor, and his respite is likely to be temporary, but he pretends that he is cured and can manage perfectly well without Lesley.

His eyesight is no handicap when it comes to composing, so he earns his living writing popular music, while remaining, at heart, a classical musician. This presentation of popular music as a cripple's alternative to the real stuff can be read as a self deprecating comment by Ivor on his own career, and the gap between his mother's ambitions and his popular, but low-brow work.

The need for popular approval ensured that the play had a happy ending, with David and Lesley back together again at the end. Meanwhile, down below, Lilian Braithwaite – who had rescued Ivor the previous year by appearing in *The Truth Game*, and as well as being one of his best friends was mother to one of Noël's, the actress, Joyce Carey, who Noël cast as the faux-genteel manager of the station buffet in *Brief Encounter* – led Viola Tree and Minnie Rayner in a comic trio whose antics broke up the intensity of the romantic struggles being played overhead. Minnie Rayner was a cockney commedienne with a long background on stage, including the First World War's long-running hit Chu Chin Chow. A complete contrast to Ivor's elegant and worldly leading ladies, he was very fond of her, and she became a mascot for him, appearing in all his plays until her death in the 1940s.

The *Morning Post* thought that Ivor's co-star, Benita Hume, stole the show: 'Even Miss Hume's triumphs on the silent and talking screen had not prepared us for anything quite so lovely and appealing' while the *Daily Telegraph* thought that the audience reaction proved that the acting honours and beauty prize, belonged to Ivor: 'When I left the New Theatre last night the audience was still playing the game of pretending that it was a hungry hyena and Mr Ivor Novello was the bone.'

102

Symphony in Two Flats transferred to New York on 30 September 1930, opening at the Sam S Shubert Theatre. The reviews were terrible, and they, together with a freak heatwave, killed it in a matter of weeks, but the theatre owners gave Ivor a second chance, largely because Billie Burke, a retired comedienne who had married Florenz Zeigfeld, had fond memories of Ivor from his holiday in New York in 1919, and was keen to appear in a Broadway version of *The Truth Game*.

The play opened at the Ethel Barrymore Theatre in late December 1930, and fared much better than *Symphony in Two Flats*. It was helped by the inevitable pleasure that New York audiences took in seeing Billie Burke on stage again – *Theatre Magazine* thought she was 'a constant ripple of joy' – but Ivor earned his fair share of praise. Picking up on the play's value as light relief after the horror of the previous year's Wall Street Crash, the *New York Times* commented that 'If matronly hearts are hungry for romance while the businessmen are computing their losses downtown, *The Truth Game* should administer to one of the primary theatrical needs...it is cute.'

Ivor and Fay Compton at a fancy dress ball, Royal Albert Hall

THE EARLY 1930s

Ivor marked the beginning of the 1930s with a film of *Symphony in Two Flats*, in which the comic relief of the lower floor was entirely cut, and in which the American version co-starred Jacqueline Logan, while the British version saw the role of Lesley played by Benita Hume, Ivor's co-star on stage and an actress more acceptable to a patriotic campaign led by the *Daily Express*, which accused Gainsborough Pictures of being pushed around by Hollywood in casting an American actress in the film of what was, undoubtedly, a British play.

Today, the soundtrack seems of very poor quality with a fairly haphazard success in synching lips movements and speech, but the 1920s-style syncopated version of Ivor's character's symphony is interesting, and it is fascinating to watch him composing on film.

Ivor's acting, though still a little theatrical for today's taste, had calmed down a lot, and the speech he makes, when he realises that Lesley has deceived him as to the outcome of the music competition, was remarkably well written, and powerfully delivered.

All of Ivor's talents – playing the piano, acting and writing – were to be used in his brief and misguided attempt to earn the proverbial fortune in Hollywood, where there was already a well established film community of British actors, whose exploits in the inter-war era has been chronicled by Sheridan Morley in *Tales from the Hollywood Raj*.

Ivor's suitability for Hollywood was challenged by an American actress, Ruth Chatterton, whose first encounter with him convinced her that he was far too refined for the place. They met at a party thrown by Clifton Webb (described by Ivor as the Jack

Buchanan of New York) in his Manhattan apartment:

'Someone pushed me to the piano, and I played Isolde's 'Liebestod.' As I sounded the last few chords I happened to look where Ruth was sitting...there were tears running down her face. She came over to the piano and, putting an arm around my shoulder, softly whispered; "You poor little boy. You play the 'Liebestod' like that and you're going to Hollywood! Never mind, perhaps I can make life pleasant for you.'

It was Ruth's idea that Ivor appear in his only film for Paramount, *Once a Lady*, in 1931. He read the script and decided that 'I hated the part, but one look into Ruth's eyes and, against my better judgement, I said I would do it. "Don't take any notice of the script, darling" said Ruth. "We'll build that part up!" Heaven knows she tried, but it was no good.'

Although the press thought Ivor looked suitably 'debonair', his initial assessment of the script was – like most of his instincts when it came to work – correct. The film was a deeply unsatisfactory one, largely due to the weakness of the plot, though the fact that it featured a train crash may have given him the idea for the spectacular train crash in his musical, *Crest of the Wave* (1937).

He also had a spell as a Hollywood scriptwriter, secured partly because of his film career as an actor, but largely because of his screen-writing and play-writing skills, and, especially, the success of *The Truth Game* in New York. The experience was, for him as for so many Hollywood writers throughout the century, an impersonal and intensely frustrating one, which in his case lasted less than a year. The problem was one of work – or lack of it – rather than California itself. He liked America, and had American friends, like the young impresario, Richard Rose, who wrote of their friendship and professional relationship (Rose had a wealthy family who funded his experiments in theatre) in *Perchance to Dream*, an entertaining memoir published in 1974.

Dreaming, on the beach or by the swimming pool, was more or less all Ivor had to do, apart from his one (largely forgotten) claim to Hollywood fame – he was scriptwriter on the first of the Tarzan movies, *Tarzan the Ape Man*. The nearest he had ever been to a jungle was in a fancy dress party at the Albert Hall, in which he was photographed, wearing a leopard skin outfit, opposite Fay

Compton. Apart from this brief excursion into cinema history, he acquired new friends and contacts, principally Greta Garbo, whom he charmed by attempting to converse with her in what remained of the Swedish that he had learned during his propaganda visit to Stockholm in 1918.

A sun lover all his life, California in some ways suited him, as it was, later, to appeal to his great friend Gladys Cooper. She had discovered sunshine, sand and the Pacific Ocean in her 50s and instantly fell in love with the Californian way of life, exchanging an English Rose complexion for the permanent tan of the dedicated sunbather. Much as Ivor enjoyed that side of Hollywood, his first love was theatre: he was keen to get back to work in the West End, wanted to see his old social circle again, and was homesick for the Aldwych flat and for Redroofs.

The studio bosses persuaded him to delay his departure for a few months but apart from making that concession – which was more a case of good manners than anything else – he remained determined to return home. One of the people that Ivor invited to his farewell party was Edgar Wallace, the crime novelist, playwright, film maker, horse racer and larger-than life, rags-to-riches character who had come, like Ivor, to Hollywood in order to boost his earning power. Wallace's contribution to Hollywood history was to be the story of *King Kong*.

On the morning of the party Wallace phoned with apologies – he had a bad cold and would not be able to come. Ivor wished him well, enjoyed the party, and the next day set off for New York, taking on the train an Alsatian dog that had wandered into his Hollywood house at what turned out to be the identical time at which his own Alsatian, to which it bore an uncanny resemblance, died in England. He gave this new dog the name of the old one: Jim.

This time Ivor's life wasn't saved by a dog, as it had been years before when he had been due to sail back on the Empress of India, but the dog's presence resulted in a strange discovery, as he later told a magazine reporter:

'His quarters were in the guard's van. At Chicago I had to change trains. I went to see how Jim was getting on. Sitting on an enormous packing case was a coloured porter checking his passenger list. Jokingly I remarked on the size of the case and added that I hoped there was no one inside. "Sure there is," said the porter. "It's a film writer who died...He's going home to England." He lifted up the label and showed me the name written on it. It was Edgar Wallace.'

Back in England, Ivor ignored the failure of his Rat sequel and made a sound version of *The Lodger* (1932), this time making his character a villain rather than a misunderstood victim. Perhaps the producers of the 1926 silent film had shown more commercial nous than Alfred Hitchcock by making the central character a hero rather than a murderer, because the talking version was a failure.

The stage provided much better results, with a play that Ivor had thought of during his months in California. *I Lived With You* is one of his two best plays (the other being *Proscenium*), and was turned into a very entertaining movie the following year (1933) which still impresses as an example of 1930s comedy and as a commentary on the English class system and the chaos wreaked when lower middle class morality is confronted, and undermined by, the whims of a foreign Royal.

Opening at the Prince of Wales Theatre on 2 March 1932, directed by Auriol Lee, the play describes how a starving Russian refugee – who happens to be a Prince – is found in the maze at Hampton Court. Though needing a decent meal, Prince Felix (Ivor) is beautifully dressed (albeit in a Russian shirt) and turns out to have on his person some fabulous family jewels – but then inner logic was never a strong point of the drawing-room comedies of this period.

The strength of the play lies in the fact that, far from taking the easy option of having the Prince rescued by a suitably grand family, Ivor's story shows the destructive effect of someone of his background and attitude being taken in by a very ordinary family in Clapham – long before the area was gentrified.

Felix's morals and his money (he gradually sells the jewels off) are, far from being admired, as would be the conventional treatment of the time, shown to be insidiously corrupting, and after a short while his presence has led to the father of the household becoming a thief (he sells the jewels for Felix, paying him far less than the sums he receives for their sale) and a womaniser with a particularly nasty mistress; his wife, deeply unhappy, turns to the bottle; the younger daughter gets ideas above her station and dumps her decent but dull boyfriend, while the older daughter, Glad, (Ursula Jeans) who had discovered Felix in the first place, has her affections trifled with by him. The only member of the family to remain unimpressed by his charm is a spinster aunt who lives with them, and is their eventual saviour by persuading Felix to leave. Some lines of Rossetti summed up the action:

And there they be
Who kissed his wings which brought him yesterday
And thank his wings to-day that he is flown.

Though happier endings were usually grafted onto plays when they transferred to the screen, Ivor felt obliged to re-write the end of *I Lived With You* within a month of it's opening. Originally, when Felix leaves, Glad rushes after him, but with no hope of ever seeing him again. In response to audience reaction, Ivor made it clear that she knew where he was heading (back to the maze) and that she would find, and keep, him. The fact that this all takes place in the context of a well-written and paced comedy that – in the film version, which is all we have left to us – shows Ivor as an accomplished comic actor as well as a romantic leading man, makes it all the more impressive as a piece of writing, and suggests that, had he continued with straight plays rather than concentrating on musicals after 1935, he might have produced some work that would have survived the last six decades instead of sinking beneath the surface glamour of the Drury Lane shows.

The other fascinating aspect of the film of *I Lived With You* is the confirmation of how dramatically Ivor's features differed between his romantic, reposed expression and when he smiled. Most photographs of Ivor in newspapers, magazines, publicity releases and books show him looking wildly handsome and alluring – every woman's dream. However, those photographs that show him smiling, particularly with his mouth open and teeth showing, transform him from moodily romantic sex symbol to camp young thing or sweet old queen – depending on his age

– in a second. Even in his last years, when age and illness had taken their toll, Ivor was strikingly handsome, but a photograph taken at a Foyles Literary Luncheon, reproduced in W MacQueen Pope's 1951 biography, shows him smiling, and therefore looking distinctly 'so' – to use a contemporary euphemism. This effect can be seen in photos throughout his life, so it must have been seen, throughout his career, by all his fans.

To his friends the fact that he was gay was, of course, no secret, but even in a more innocent age than our own the fact was plainly there for those who wanted to see it. His female fans, of course, did not want to see it, and so ignored it. Given that one woman, congratulating him on his performance in *The Rat* in 1924, had said "You looked so lovely when you spat!" it is not surprising, perhaps, that the fact that his smile radiated camp was simply taken as evidence of charming high spirits.

On the positive side, the moments when his face is caught, and almost frozen, by the camera during *I Lived With You* equally demonstrate the potency of his sex appeal which was unaffected by the effeminacy so frequently commented on by his earlier film critics (and taken to heart by American audiences, if not British ones). There is one moment, in particular, when he is in the Clapham house's best room, wearing a Russian silk shirt, where the combination of his looks and the camera angle (not, for once, a profile shot) produce a sudden burst of sheer beauty that is simply breathtaking.

If, *Cinema Paradiso* style, one were to make a collection of moments in film – lasting a mere two or three seconds each – when an actor's beauty (male as well as female) almost literally stops the show, then Novello would be up there along with Garbo. It is, perhaps, this shared sense of their effect on a cinema audience that drew them together as much as anything else, and when on one occasion, in the late 1940s, Ivor gave a private showing of one of his earliest films, *The White Rose*, and asked Garbo, who was in his party, what she thought of his performance, she immediately (and tactfully) replied "You were so beautiful!"

While Ivor was still performing in the stage version of *I Lived With You* at the Prince of Wales Theatre, another of his plays,

Ivor and Ursula Jeans in I Lived With You, 1932

Party, starring Lilian Braithwaite and Benita Hume, enjoyed a run at the Strand Theatre, in the Aldwych (and underneath his flat). The play describes a party at the home of an actress, Miranda Clayfoot (a morally descriptive name in the fashion of Restoration characters) whose drug habit has exacerbated her naturally impetuous behaviour. She throws the party as an excuse to seduce her ex lover, Bay Clender (Ivor), who is now happily married. The other main character is that of an ageing star with a splendid, vicious, wit, Mrs MacDonald. Her temperament and Celtic surname are both hints (as if they were needed) that the character was obviously based on Mrs Patrick Campbell, the Edwardian beauty beloved of George Bernard Shaw who had let herself go and was described as resembling a sinking battleship (she had become very stout) determinedly firing on her rescuers. Lilian Braithwaite threw herself into the role of Mrs MacDonald with gusto, while Benita Hume looked deceptively sweet as Miranda.

Party lived up to its name and was as much a cabaret as a play, with various star turns performing their party pieces, in order to make what had originally been a very short curtain-raiser into a piece long enough to stand on its own. The *Observer* noted the lack of structure: 'There is a bit of a plot, which is only a polite salute to the conventions of play-making, and a studio entertainment is included...' but the *Daily Telegraph* begged to differ: ' The whole affair is, in fact, an elaborate and happy jest by the theatrical world at its own expense. But so that the public shall not find itself left out of a family joke, there is a story which binds the whole affair together and turns what might otherwise have been a brilliant charade into a play.'

Whether or not it could really qualify as a play, it was certainly a hit, with the *Morning Post* recording a 'tempest of applause' and the *Daily Mail* a 'wildly uproarious, deliciously enthusiastic reception.'

1933 began with *Fresh Fields*, which opened at the Criterion Theatre, on Piccadilly Circus, on 5 January, to equally good audience response. One of Ivor's most successful plays, it was inspired by his mascot, Minnie Rayner. Ivor had given her an open invitation to go down to Redroofs, which she had taken up, arriving without warning but with a large group of friends, one Sunday afternoon. Ivor's play deals with an aristocratic woman, Lady Lilian Bedworthy (another Restoration surname), who lives in a vast Belgravia mansion with her sister, the widowed Lady Mary Crabbe. Lady Mary decides to take in paying guests, in the form of an Australian family, the Pidgeons – creating plenty of comic potential for culture shocks as well as class differences. Lady Mary does not want Lady Lilian, who earns some money writing a newspaper column called 'Can I help you?' – shades of William Boot in Evelyn Waugh's *Scoop* – to know about this arrangement, part of which is that the Pidgeon's daughter is to be presented at Court by another aristocrat, Lady Strawholme (played by Martita Hunt).

The comic potential in the situation is obvious, and one scene – whose double entendre seems fairly tame today – brought the house down. Una, the daughter, has broken a vase, and she describes to Lady Lilian how she has got into trouble and wants her help in getting rid of it (the broken vase). Lady Lilian assumes that the 'trouble' is pregnancy and is horrified. The exchange had the audience in stitches, and on one memorable occasion Queen Mary, who was a great fan of Ivor's work, brought her brother, the Earl of Athlone, to see the play from the royal box. The management were appalled at the possibility of the Queen listening to sexual innuendo, but Ivor refused to cut the lines (he was good at standing up to producers when necessary) and Her Majesty and the Earl were seen convulsed with mirth when the scene occurred.

Queen Mary has a reputation as an unbendingly stern figurehead and although it is true that she was far more at ease with the role of Queen than of mother, and shared, with her husband, a Victorian attitude towards protocol, she had a charming smile and infectious laugh, and greatly enjoyed meeting theatre stars, usually receiving them in the royal retiring room behind the royal box in the interval of the show she was visiting. This could have unfortunate consequences, as when Vivien Leigh and Robert Helpmann, in costume as Oberon and Titania, backed out of the Queen's presence, bowing and curtseying, and got their fairy crowns (they were still in stage costume) entangled.

On another occasion an actress was so flustered at being in the Queen's presence that she backed humbly out of the retiring room – but through the wrong door. To her horror she discovered she had backed, not into the corridor, but into the royal lavatory, from where she was rescued, blushing furiously, by a more clear-headed colleague. Jessica James, who played Maria Ziegler, the female

A rehearsal reading of Proscenium, 1933 (Fay Compton seated, left foreground)

lead in *The Dancing Years* at the London Casino (now the Prince Edward Theatre) during the 1940s, was presented to Queen Mary. The Queen was very friendly, addressed her as 'Dear gel' and expressed admiration for the way she swept around the stage in her exquisite gowns with long satin trains.

Fresh Fields gave the Queen not only an opportunity to laugh but a happy ending, with Miss Pidgeon marrying Lady Mary's son (played by Bobbie Andrews) and her uncle, a rugged Australian with a heart of gold and a large bank balance, marrying Lady

114

Lilian. The Sunday Dispatch thought 'It screams success from the word go' and the *Daily Telegraph* thought the play an example of Ivor's ability to provide 'excellent entertainment' and 'very funny', opinions that were shared by the public; but when the play reached New York, in 1936 (with an American cast) it was not well received. Ivor's work never really appealed to an American audience – on home territory, at least: many Anglophile American visitors saw and enjoyed his plays and musicals in London.

Ivor had decided against writing a part for himself in *Fresh Fields*, perhaps to avoid stealing Bobbie's thunder, so he saved his

Ivor snuggles up to Fay Compton, Proscenium, 1933

acting energies for *Flies in the Sun* (The Playhouse, 13 January), a tale of the idle rich in the South of France which failed to appeal to the London public. One reason for its unpopularity was that Ivor had written a more direct indictment of upper class morals (or their lack) than in *I Lived With You*, and his audience made it clear than they were determined to be charmed rather than challenged, and wanted him to go back to the previous mixture of romance and laughter. If they wanted a playwright to be acerbic, they'd go to see a Coward show. Ivor was supposed to be lovely, not laconic, and he resigned himself to his fate:

'I'm sure I'll always have to write romantic parts for myself. That's what the audience wants and that's the only way I can have a success.'

The most entertaining review of the play came in the *Times*, which hoped against hope that:

'in his parade of presumably popular effects, the dramatist has had his tongue in his cheek...There is suicide and song; there is a lady's maid in hysterics, and there are little jokes of all sorts...Much of the furniture is decorative, and when anyone dives into the sea, one hears the hopeful splash. Unhappily they can all swim.'

Far worse reviews greeted The *Sunshine Sisters*, another of Ivor's plays to open (and close) in 1933, an astonishingly productive year that showed how much he had missed London during his period in California, and how well he had used his enforced leisure to work out plots and characterisation for new plays.

That his productivity was not always matched by quality control is proved by the reception given to The *Sunshine Sisters*, which was a frothy piece starring Phylis Monkman, Dorothy Dickson (later to be one of his great leading ladies at Drury Lane) and Joan Clarkson. In the play a music-hall trio of three beautiful sisters, whose surname is Sunshine (a typical Novello touch) are picked up in Paris by a young man (played by Jack Hawkins, a Novello regular in the early 1930s) and taken back home to mummy. This being the 1930s and a Novello play, mummy turns out to be a Duchess with a Gladstonian habit of rescuing and reforming waifs and strays. Knowing her penchant for helping fallen women, the lad tells his mother the girls are all prostitutes, working as a family, but of course he does not inform the girls of this deception. This leads to a one-joke play that is distinctly below the standards Ivor had set himself in *Fresh Fields* and *I Lived With You*.

It's failure was pointed up by the success, at the Globe Theatre, Shaftesbury Avenue, of what proved to be one of his best plays, *Proscenium*, which was set, as its title implies, in a theatre. He opened the play with a prologue, set in the First World War, in which he played a middle-aged army officer (Colonel Sir Geoffrey Bethel) who loves a young actress, Norma Matthews, (played by Fay Compton) but who is married and therefore not free to be with her in the way that he would like. Photographs of Ivor in the role show him made up to look remarkably like his father, who had died of a heart attack in 1931, as Ivor was to do, twenty years after him. In a newspaper interview Ivor said that 'the appearance and manners of the Colonel are based on my dear father who died two years ago when I was 4000 miles away.'

The play then moves on to the present (ie 1933), with Norma, now herself nearly forty, married to an actor, Gray Raynor, (Ivor) ten years her junior. His mother, Lady Raynor, (played by Zena Dare, an Edwardian beauty whom Ivor had tempted out of retirement – she had married an aristocrat) disapproves of the match, and lets slip the fact that Gray is her son by her first husband – the army officer, Sir Geoffrey, whom Norma had loved, but who had died at the Front.

Along with the inevitable angst that this causes her (with a delicious irony Sir Geoffrey had, at their last dinner together, said that he hoped she would one day meet his son, and become friends with him) Norma is worried that she is growing too old for her career and for her marriage. Their theatre company is supposed to be mounting a production of *Romeo and Juliet*, and Norma is distressed at the fact that she is now too old to play Juliet – and her quip about not being quite old enough for the nurse is born of bitterness rather than humour.

The theatre critic of the *Sunday Referee* thought he detected a Freudian sub-text to Norma's worries about her age, and that this was a displacement of Ivor's own anxiety about turning forty. The idea is an interesting one, and worth quoting:

'In Ivor Novello's *Proscenium*, the new play at the Globe, the author makes his appearance in a prologue disguised as a fifty years old colonel. With greyed hair and carefully toned voice he suits the character admirably. For the rest of the evening he plays this man's son, who is twenty-six, and the previous scene by contrast helps him to look the part. But he is clearly not that age. Well preserved, but no longer young. And a reference book informs us that Ivor Novello was born in 1893. Well, what is forty to a successful actor or to anyone else except to those with a Peter Pan complex? But forty seems to be worrying Novello, for at the bottom of his play, and on too much of its surface, is the feeling that youth is passing, and it is all very sad and is not to be borne.'

If the reviewer thought that Ivor was pushing his luck playing a twenty-six year old (and he was to continue playing even younger parts for another decade) one can imagine his reaction to the excerpt from *Romeo and Juliet*, where he was playing a seventeen year old boy.

The *Romeo and Juliet* production, while being germane to the plot, was also a self-indulgent device whereby Ivor was able to play Romeo on stage - an ambition of his for many years. Although he could get away with playing Romeo as a young man, rather than a teenager, he was not most people's idea of suitable casting in the part. As the Gielgud/Olivier production was to prove two years later, most people thought a lustily heterosexual Romeo (Olivier) was preferable to a more poetic, gentle version (Gielgud). Ivor's performance, though heartfelt, was not his best, and if the poses he struck in the production photographs are anything to go by, his playing of the part would have made Gielgud's seem positively butch.

Romeo and Juliet also allowed a sub-plot about a scheming minx of a young actress with designs on Gray's body. So depressed does Norma become that when her female intuition picks up the girl's interest in her husband, she not only fails to fight her corner, she positively encourages her, throwing them together at rehearsals with phrases like "I'll leave you two young things together." Gray is entirely unmoved by Eunice's advances, much to her fury, and remains faithful to Norma, so the play ends on a happy note.

One of the characters in *Proscenium* is an American producer, to whom Ivor gave a speech which expressed his own attitude to drama. It is worth quoting here, both as an expression of his love of theatre, spoken on stage in a play set in a theatre, and for the way that it parallels the speech he later gave to Rudi Kleber, his character in *The Dancing Years*, though Rudi's speech was an adaptation of this one, and referred to music rather than play-writing:

'I believe in the theatre – I believe in beauty in the theatre – I believe that in the theatre lies a road back to sanity – that the road will only be found through endeavour – the highest standard – nothing but the best. I want to give people the chance to dream again – and I want to show them that there is an art beyond the reach of mechanical devices and black and white shadows chasing each other round a white sheet...'

Whatever his feelings about cinema as an art form compared to theatre, it is surprising, given the quality of the writing and the production, that Ivor didn't film *Proscenium*. His reservations about the silver screen did not, after all, prevent him from making the (talking) film of *I Lived With You* in 1933, and in the same year he starred opposite Madeleine Carroll – who a few years later was to bring a touch of erotic glamour to Hitchcock's film of John Buchan's thriller, The *Thirty-Nine Steps* – in a film comedy called *Sleeping Car*.

Ivor's last film, in 1934, did see him appear opposite Fay Compton, his stage partner in *Proscenium*, but in a dreadful film, *Autumn Crocus*. In it Fay played an old maid, Jenny, whose holiday (her travelling companion is another teacher, of distinctly lesbian appearance) in the mountains of the Austrian Tyrol leads to an intense romance with a hotel owner, Steiner, played by Ivor. It is a poor man's Now Voyager which ends, not with the moon and the stars, but with the frustrated but plucky Fay teaching her schoolchildren a Tyrolean folk song.

Directed by Basil Dean, with a screenplay by Dorothy Farnum, adapted from the highly successful play by Dodie Smith, *Autumn Crocus*, viewed today, is embarrassingly bad. In particular, Ivor's performance is atrocious: over the top, saccharine and insincere. If his performance in *Sirocco* had been anything as poor as his portrayal of Steiner in *Autumn Crocus*, one would have sided with the rioters in the gallery at Daly's. The film is chiefly of (very minor) interest because of it's use of future talent – Basil Dean was assisted by the young Carol Reed, while one half of a young couple was played by Jack Hawkins. The minor characters also provide some of the humour, such as the vicar brother of a nosy spinster, who gets drunk on Austrian beer.

Given Ivor's inherent romanticism and gallantry towards women, he presumably found the role of a heartless, superficial seducer entirely unsympathetic, but that would be a reason for him to turn the part down rather than murder it on screen. One episode that would have appealed to him when he read the script was a balcony scene that has distinct echoes of *Romeo and Juliet*

– a favourite play of Fay's character, and, as has already been commented on in reference to *Proscenium*, a play that Ivor was always keen to appear in.

Fay Compton, by contrast, made the most of her – admittedly much more sympathetic, and interesting – part, and shows considerable acting skill. Her character is meant to be thirty-five but, while hoping for romance with Ivor, pretends to be twenty-nine. Viewing her performance in the same frame as Ivor's merely serves to show his bad acting up all the more. It is generally assumed that he gave up making films because he wanted to concentrate on his musicals, but it may be that he was sufficiently embarrassed by this effort to throw in the towel at that point. The makers of the film seemed to be equally ashamed, and it ends with a billowing Union Jack and the legend 'A British Film'.

There had already been a xenophobic thread running through the film – that the Continent was never as clean as England – and this final, desperate appeal to patriotism, in the hope that jingoistic sentiment would drown any artistic judgement, seems particularly ill-judged. It is a great shame that Ivor's film career, which included some as entertaining as Call of the Blood, *The Lodger* and *I Lived With You*, should have ended on so bathetic a note.

1934, the year of *Autumn Crocus*, saw Ivor starring in yet another of his plays, this time a thriller with the enticing title of *Murder in Mayfair*. The plot was well-written, the cast (which included Fay Compton, Edna Best, Zena Dare and Bobbie Andrews) were elegant, the director was an intelligent and accomplished German woman, Leontine Sagan, whose ability with *Murder in Mayfair* was to land her the job of directing *Glamorous Night* at Drury Lane the following year, and the set and costumes were chic.

The *Daily Telegraph* attacked him for attempting to write a thriller – on the grounds that it required rather more effort and skill than the comedies for which he was better known: 'Mr Novello is an excellent confectioner of airy trifles, but he simply cannot tackle reality, and would be well advised to recognise the fact and stop trying.'

Given the nature of his plot, this criticism seems very far wide of the mark, for although the play involves a murder, and drugs,

Ivor's treatment is far from being grittily realistic. The story concerns Jacques Clavel, a talented French pianist (giving Ivor the chance to demonstrate his musical talent before a paying audience) who falls for a married woman – and, this being a Novello play, we are not surprised to learn that she is not just married, she's a Duchess. Realising he can't persuade her to leave her husband, he marries a ghastly little minx, Auriol Crannock (Edna Best). After many years Jacques and the Duchess (Fay Compton) meet again at a party. The Duchess is now a widow, while Auriol has turned out to be an addict whose drug habit has wrecked Jacques's life and fortune. The party proves to be a disaster, and later that night Auriol is shot dead. Jacques is immediately suspected but Auriol's lover (Bobbie Andrews) proves to be the real assassin, and Jacques is free to marry his Duchess.

The *Sunday Times* thought that Bobbie Andrews had been seen too often in the West End, boyishly charming and tennis racket in hand, for him to be convincing as a drug abuser's boyfriend, let alone a murderer. The *Daily Telegraph* loved the play, reserving special praise for its author and star, defending his acting ability from sterner critics:

'See him in his present thriller, *Murder in Mayfair*. Note the consistency of his portraiture, his nervous sincerity and concentration, how he acts with every one of his fingers, how every mood of the temperamental foreign pianist works itself out to perfection, and how subordinate he can be when the situation calls for deference to the other player.'

Ivor's consideration for others, on and off stage, was called on during the pre-London tour of *Murder in Mayfair*, when Zena Dare's husband died. Ivor was phoned by her butler (stars had that sort of lifestyle in those days) and told of his death. As she was appearing on stage at any moment, Ivor decided not to tell her. As soon as the curtain calls finished Ivor took her aside and broke the news. After the funeral she realised that his suggestion – that it would help her to come back to work as soon as possible – was right and she did so, staying at Redroofs, at his suggestion, for a couple of months while she looked for a new home.

The last peacetime plays that Ivor wrote were, appropriately, comedies. The first, opening at the Theatre Royal, Haymarket

Ivor and Zena Dare, Murder in Mayfair 1934

on 25 August 1935 was *Full House*, in which he did not appear but in which the Novello standard was borne with customary panache by Lilian Braithwaite, Isabel Jeans and Bobbie Andrews. The plot, like *Fresh Fields*, concerned an aristocratic woman whose sister is trying to make ends meet – in this case by turning the house into an illicit casino. The sister, played by Isabel Jeans, at one point wrestles with her husband's mistress, played by a glamorous blond, Heather Thatcher (no relation!) and puts her over her knee and spanks her.

The fact that this was a variation on *Fresh Fields*, with the same leading lady, and Bobbie Andrews reprising his as the male love interest, was picked up on by the press, with the *Observer* suspecting Ivor had written it in a week, and the *Daily Telegraph* wearily commenting:

'Miss Braithwaite does all that is possible with the leading part. She brings her own brilliant sense of fun to the character. There is nothing else to say about her performance; we have seen it so often before.'

The play does, however, have a lot of humour, was easy on the eye in a stylish Art Deco way, and the spanking scene alone ensured that ticket sales slid the production comfortably into profit. The sight of Miss Thatcher's bottom being spanked may have led to more gentlemen of a certain sort sliding into the dress circle, for there was an electric sense of sex in the air during that scene.

In a sense Ivor sold out half way through the play, or at least as far as Miss Thatcher's character, Lady April Hannington, is concerned. At the beginning of the play she is a lively, independent woman, but by the end she falls, routinely, for the juvenile love interest in a way that the woman she is portrayed as being at the start never would.

Another case of Ivor's facile treatment of a character because it made his work as the playwright easier (and, to be fair, gave his public what they expected) was Mr Rosenblatt, a Jewish character whom the audience is meant to laugh at (and did) for the way he pronounced his 'w's as 'v's, and frequently exclaimed "Oi!Oi!Oi!" This was not a case of Ivor being anti-Semitic, which he never was – on the contrary, see *The Dancing Years* – but it was an example of him taking a stock comic figure, which might as easily have been a Scotsman or a Frenchman, rather than working on a subtler presentation of a character.

The last of his peacetime plays (as an author, and, as with *Full House*, in which he did not appear) was *Comedienne*, which starred, yet again, the redoubtable Lilian Braithwaite. In a role crafted with her in mind, and partly modelled (as in *Party*) on Mrs Patrick Campbell, the play tells the story with sub plots that feed into the main action – of an ageing actress, once very beautiful and grand, living in retirement in a friend's flat, attended by her faithful old dresser (played by Kathleen Harrison, whose career took off after the Second World War, with a leading role, alongside Jack Warner, in *Holiday Camp*). Lilian Braithwaite's character, Donna Lovelace, is a monster of ingratitude who seems fuelled by bitterness and malice, yet despite her ghastly (and self-destructive) behaviour has something admirable about her, a largeness of spirit – if not a very kind one – which harks back to an age when leading ladies had to be larger than life, and when starry behaviour, allied to a waspish wit, was their only defence in a glamorous but often hostile environment.

The *Times* thought that 'Mr Novello's study of Donna Lovelace herself is of genuine value both as entertainment and as illuminating comment on the theatre...' while the *Daily Telegraph* thought it 'the best play he has written, certainly his best backstage piece. It may not prove his most financially successful one, but it represents decidedly the most artistic work of his career...[it] bristles throughout with genuine wit.'

Even those who thought the play had its weaknesses, admitted that with Lilian Braithwaite in the lead role it was bound to do well:

'In all probability the amusingness of the character will triumph over the slackness of the story. There is the risk that the average audience may tire of listening to so much theatrical 'shop' but Lilian Braithwaite does most of the talking, and that must reduce the risk.'

Ivor appeared in two more peacetime shows (*The Happy Hypocrite* and *Henry V*) which belong, chronologically, in the chapters on his Drury Lane years, but it seems appropriate to feature them here, among his peactime plays rather than among his musicals.

The Happy Hypocrite, which opened at His Majesty's Theatre, in the Haymarket, on 8 April 1936, is chiefly remembered today for the fact that it was the second West End appearance for the young, and relatively unknown, Vivien Leigh. Ivor had first met her when she unsuccessfully auditioned (along with Coral Browne and Sally Gray) for a part in *Murder in Mayfair*. Although she had not been cast, Ivor recognised her beauty, which was fairly obvious, and her talent, which was less clear at that stage. He promised her that he would follow her career with interest, and write a good role for her in another play. With most playwrights that would just have been a tactful way of dismissing her, but Ivor was always as good as his word, and cast her as the love interest in *The Happy Hypocrite*.

Although this was the only occasion on which he was to work with her, they became great friends, and he took an affectionate interest in her career, and provided a refuge – at Redroofs and in Jamaica – when she needed one. He always claimed that it was he who had persuaded her to change her name, from Vivian Hartley to Vivien Leigh, feminising her Christian name and using her husband's Christian name (he was a barrister called Leigh Holman) as a surname. Rosemary Geddes, who was Vivien Leigh's private secretary and friend for the last seven years of her life, contradicts Ivor's account (which he gave to Vanessa Lee in the 1940s) and says that it was Vivien's manager, not Ivor, who had suggested the name.

What is not in dispute is that her first West End appearance had been the previous year, 1935, in *The Mask of Virtue*, and that *The Happy Hypocrite* also had a mask as its theme.

The play was taken from a short story by the writer and wit Max Beerbohm (whose half brother had built Her Majesty's Theatre), and been dramatised by Richard Addinsell and Clemence Dane. The essential premise of the story is that we all, in a metaphorical sense, wear masks. We present an image to the world that we have created. We want the world to see us as we would like to be seen, but our literal masks – our faces – take on the attributes that most faithfully reflect our characters – thus defeating our attempts at concealment.

Ivor played a Regency rake, appropriately named Lord George Hell, whose dissolute and debauched life is etched, horribly, on his face. Ivor supposedly wanted to play the role because he didn't want to be judged on his famously good looks, but this was disingenuous of him, as the play's plot meant that despite an initially ghastly appearance his good looks would have plenty of opportunity to be shown to an adoring audience as the action progressed, and also because the very fact of his boyish appearance and perfect profile being submerged in (clever and effective) make-up made for wonderful free publicity in 'How It Is Done' articles in the press.

Lord George goes to the theatre one evening and falls in love with an actress, Jenny Mere, played by Vivien Leigh. He falls in love because Eros, the God of Love, played by a young, slim and attractive Marius Goring wearing winged sandals and little else, fires his arrow at the miserable reprobate as he leers at Jenny from the comfort of his box.

Lord George duly falls for Jenny, but although he has lost his heart, he retains his reason, and is all too well aware that a beautiful young woman will not enjoy being courted by a raddled old rake like himself. Accordingly he pops into a convenient mask shop and decides to buy one, which covers most of his face (in a sort of precursor to *The Phantom of the Opera*). The mask, by a happy coincidence, is of Ivor's face.

Thus armed, Lord George makes quick headway with Jenny, but his previous mistress, played by Isabel Jeans, (a strikingly attractive actress who excelled in chic and worldly roles) irritated at being scorned, decides to literally unmask him for the fraud he is, and tears the deceptive facade away. To her fury and the audience's intense pleasure, the mask is ripped off to reveal – Ivor's face. A challenge to the make-up department as well as theatre-goers' credulity, the moral of this is that we get the face we deserve, and, thanks to the love of a good woman, Lord George's character has been completely reformed, so his inner beauty is now reflected his handsome looks.

Thus transformed, he sweeps Jenny off to a country cottage where he tends the earth with a heart-shaped spade, and they live, in a rural idyll, happily ever after.

The show's plot was as ludicrous as it sounds, and despite Ivor's presence, the combined beauty of Misses Leigh and Jeans, and superb sets by Motley, the female team who also designed plays for John Gielgud, it ran for only a few weeks, but it had the merit of confirming Vivien Leigh as an up-and-coming star who, according to the *Sunday Times*, was 'artless without artifice, and no simper mars this freshness and this calm.' Ivor was praised for the depth of his acting, but many critics saw through the apparent difficulty of labouring under unattractive make up, and poked fun at the final transformation, with the *Sunday Pictorial*, for example, referring to how Miss Leigh complimented him on the 'full glory' of his face.

The play did, however, reflect Ivor's new enthusiasm for musical theatre, as it combined straight drama with music and dance. The Regency setting was recycled, nine years later, for *Perchance to Dream*, to much better effect than in *The Happy Hypocrite*. The show's failure left Ivor undaunted, and he threw himself into working on his next musical, *Careless Rapture*, which was booked for Drury Lane.

After both *Careless Rapture* (1936) and *Crest of the Wave* (1937), Ivor wanted to try his luck with a straight play at Drury Lane. The theatre was too vast for any of his own plays, and in any case he wanted to prove himself a serious actor, so to most people's surprise he decided to play Shakespeare. Although this had two practical benefits – he didn't have to go to the trouble of writing a new play, and there were no copyright payments to be made to the author – it was a considerable critical risk.

He would have been better suited to play a gentler, more romantic role, but the two that would have suited him most, Hamlet and Richard II, had both been played, to perfection, by John Gielgud, who had re-enforced his claim to Richard II by playing him not just in Shakespeare, but in Gordon Daviot's popular *Richard of Bordeaux*.

Even so, *Henry V* has, historically, been seen as a curious choice for Ivor to make. A ruggedly masculine and warlike part, it seemed unlikely to show him to his best advantage, but the more one looks at it the more apparent it was why he tried the role. In

Ivor thinking of 'The Land Of Might Have Been'

the first place Henry was a Welshman, and the play stresses this more than the history books ever have. Ivor's Welsh lilt, which he never lost despite all the years he spent in England and the Unites States, was ideally suited for the role.

Henry V is set in the middle ages, and the opportunities for spectacle and glamour seemed ideal for Drury Lane, and Ivor's production was a typically lavish one. It is, too, a notably patriotic play, with the wonderful speech with which Henry rallies his troops:

> We few, we happy few, we band of brothers;
> For he to-day that sheds his blood with me
> Shall be my brother; be he ne'er so vile
> This day shall gentle his condition:
> And gentlemen in England, now a-bed
> Shall think themselves accursed they were not here,
> And hold their manhoods cheap whiles any speaks
> That fought with us upon St Crispin's Day.

Ivor put the show on at a time of gathering international tension, and although his interest in politics was negligible – unless it affected culture, in which case he was stung into action, as with *The Dancing Years* – he must have thought that a patriotic play about a just war on the continent would have an immediate, and profitable, appeal to a London audience.

The other element that would appeal to him was the comedy in the play. The wooing scene between the King and Princess Katherine is an entertaining episode, and Ivor's talents were well suited to the charm and humour the lines require. Despite this, and the presence of a 'serious' actress, Gwen Ffrangcon-Davies as Chorus, the critics were not overly impressed, and audiences failed to materialise.

The *Observer* took issue with the production's over-the-top pageantry: 'The play is here in danger of foundering under its own load of hard ware...There never was more glittering parade of weapons, never armies more terrible with steel and brilliant with banners.' Although Ivor gave 'a modest and careful and well-graced performance...This Harry is not naturally rhetorical...His best speeches are his quiet ones, the reflections on Ceremony and conversation with the private soldiers.'

This being a Novello show, there was a lot of incidental music, which the *Bystander* considered 'excellent', but the play's the thing and it was generally agreed that, however poetic Ivor could be, his was not a memorable version of the play. The public stayed away in droves. Ivor wrote to a friend that 'It is a comfort to know that though *Henry V* was a financial disaster, people really did love it', but those that did tended to be friends and die-hard fans who would have loved anything he appeared in. Even the appeal to patriotism backfired, in that people were more keen on getting home and listening to the radio (this was the time of the Munich Crisis) and worrying about the possibilities of a second twentieth century war than paying to see a production of a play about an early fifteenth century one.

Ivor's characteristic response to failure was to organise a fresh success, which he did by writing *The Dancing Years*, the most popular stage show of the Second World War, and the last of the Drury Lane musicals that had begun, at a lunch at The Ivy, back in 1934.

Ivor and Mary Ellis enjoy their gypsy wedding in Glamorous Night, 1935

GLAMOROUS NIGHT

In 1934 the Theatre Royal, Drury Lane, was in a mess. The theatre was huge, and needed an appropriately large-scale production to fill it, but since Noël Coward's *Cavalcade* in 1931, and with the exception of the crowd-pleasing pantomimes regularly booked every year, the place had failed to find a money-spinning show. Despite it's long and illustrious pedigree and the prestige of holding the royal warrant, it looked probable that Drury Lane would have to close. The final indignity would be for it to be converted into a cinema.

Harry Tennent managed the theatre on behalf of its Board of Directors, and also ran H M Tennent, a theatre agency which, under his business partner, Hugh 'Binkie' Beaumont – a Welshman who came from the same part of Cardiff as Ivor – was to dominate the West End from the late 1930s to the late 1950s. Tennent knew of Ivor's musical background, and, in desperation, asked him to lunch at the Ivy to see if he might be able to come up with an idea for a show.

Only a couple of years before, Ivor, in one of his newspaper interviews, had spoken of his mother's old, and frustrated, ambition: 'She has a dream, which I fear will never be fulfilled – that of seeing my own opera at Covent Garden.'

She, it seems, was not the only one: 'Hardly a day passes but someone asks me, in a voice choked with sentiment, "What has become of your music?"'

At the time, he claimed to have put professional composing behind him: 'The days have long since gone when I had to think "I've got to turn out some tunes this week or the rent won't get paid." My conviction is that unless a talent can be regarded as being the real thing in one's life, so that it blots out everything else, then that talent is best left alone. That's what happened to my music. I get more enjoyment now when I sit at the piano and improvise with no thought of publication, than I ever got when I was under the necessity of writing tinkling tunes for money.

Also – financially speaking – a thing like 'Home Fires' only happens once. As a composer of at least seven musical plays I can with heartfelt feeling assure those people who think that a composer of light opera in England must surely become a millionaire that they haven't 'read the programme!'"

Whatever his public protestations, Harry knew that Ivor was still fascinated by music, that he was a regular at the Royal Opera House, Covent Garden, and that he lapped up new musicals as eagerly as he did the latest plays and films.

Harry needed to fill Drury Lane if he was going to save it, and of all the major players in West End theatre, Ivor was the man with the most consistently popular touch. Coward's *Cavalcade* had been a marvellous and patriotic pageant, but what was needed now was something more romantic, and with good tunes.

Ivor, touched by Harry Tennent's faith in him, appalled at the idea of Drury Lane's closure and thrilled at the prospect of being given carte blanche to save it, improvised his plans for a show. As the waiters cleared away the main course and prepared to bring on the dessert – Ivor later had one specially named after him (an ice-cream called Bombe Ivor Novello) at the Ivy's sister restaurant, the Caprice – he improvised.

He had a plan for a royal romance, gypsy weddings, murder, ocean liners, shipwrecks (Harry gulped, but nodded when Ivor said he was sure that Drury Lane's technical team would be able to produce the desired effect), an opera star, a palace ballroom scene, an enormous cast and an orchestra. He drew on all the operettas he had ever seen, the notorious and newsworthy romance between Madame Lupescu and the King of Romania, and his own vivid, extraordinary imagination. As he finally finished, in a haze of smoke from the Turkish cigarettes he had chain smoked since he had first had to smoke, on stage, in *The Rat* ten years earlier, there was a brief pause before Harry said: "Splendid. Of course, the Board will have to approve, so would you be able to let them see the synopsis tomorrow?" Ivor, who had bluffed Harry into thinking the show was written and waiting in the proverbial drawer for an impresario to back it, agreed – he had no other choice.

The next twenty-four hours were spent in a whirlwind of activity, fuelled by the inevitable cigarettes and gallons of black coffee. Not only was his reputation on the line, he was determined to prove that Drury Lane didn't have to go to America in order to find a large-scale musical to fill its vast auditorium.

The board – who were, admittedly, pretty desperate – accepted his synopsis, and he then had the relative luxury of writing the show in a couple of weeks. He was helped by the fact that he was able to use several tunes that he had already composed but not found an outlet for, by the fact that he had a mind full of tunes in any case, able to produce music with an extraordinary facility when called upon to do so, and, finally, by his choice of lyricist, a young poet and would-be-actor called Christopher Hassall.

Ivor had spotted Chris Hassall when he had been hired as a juvenile for one of Ivor's plays. His dark hair and good looks made him suitable as an understudy, but in addition to not being up to playing lead roles with any great confidence, he had the double disadvantage of not being good at learning his lines. When Ivor was accidentally injured one day, he had to confess that he wasn't up to going on in his place, so Ivor had to stagger on, regardless.

Many actor-managers would have sacked him on the spot, but Ivor took pity on him, and was sufficiently approachable for Hassall to feel able to show him some of his poetry – though this may have been a tactic for persuading Ivor that he was too interesting a man to simply dismiss for not learning his lines properly. Ivor, in turn, introduced him to Sir Edward Marsh, his old friend and cultural mentor, and Marsh took an immediate shine to him. This was because of his looks as much as his budding talents, and though this third protégé was not in the same cultural or physical league as Rupert Brooke or Ivor Novello, he became very fond of him, helping him both financially and with career advice and introductions. Hassall later repaid the debt by writing an informative biography of Sir Edward that is still worth reading today.

Ivor and Chris Hassall worked together extremely well, and the effectiveness of the songs owes much to the strength and charm of Hassall's lyrics. These were often kicked off, as it were, by Ivor, who as well as providing the tune would often suggest it's title (as in *Glamorous Night*, the title of the musical itself) or the first few words.

By the middle of October, 1934, the script and score of the musical was ready. What was essential, of course, was a cast that could do the show justice. Ivor would play the lead, in a non-singing role – which then as now was highly unusual. One of reason why his shows have not been professionally revived is that all the best songs are for women, with men's solos being given to minor roles rather than the leading man.

In *Glamorous Night* there is a good part for a tenor, and Ivor cast Trefor Jones, a fellow Welshman. The Welsh were also represented, among the main female parts, by Olive Gilbert, who had sung with the Carl Rosa Opera Company, and was to be one of his most stalwart character actresses and singers, and a great personal friend, who lived in the flat below his in the Aldwych.

Although he had been determined to write and star in a British show, his ambition had been motivated (apart from reasons of personal glory) by a healthy patriotism rather than anti-Americanism. His enjoyment of the social and cultural resources of New York has already been referred to, and he admired many American singers. One, in particular, he thought would be ideal: Mary Ellis.

Mary Ellis, who died in 2003, aged 105 had sung solo roles at the New York Met during the First World War, created the role of *Rose Marie* on Broadway, and enjoyed a career both in 'straight' theatre (including Shakespeare) and on film. She was also remarkably beautiful, and thus had the very rare combination of wonderful looks, genuine acting talent and a voice that was good – and versatile – enough for both opera and stage musicals. Ivor had seen her, the previous year, in Jerome Kern's *Music in the Air*, and had, as usual with actresses he admired, offered to write a show for her.

It was obvious that Ivor needed a woman to play his love interest. What was radical, however, was in having a woman director

136

In Ivor's shows love never came easy...with Fay Compton

– Leontine Sagan. A south African who later returned there to found South Africa's equivalent of the National Theatre, she had come to prominence in London a couple of years earlier, when she had directed 'Children in Uniform', a play set in a girl's academy.

Ivor saw that she had the flair, imagination, and ability to impose discipline (she was quickly christened Madame Hitler by the performers) on a very large cast and the far-from docile stage hands. In the mid 1930s (*Glamorous Night* opened on 2 May 1935)

Ivor liked to sleep in, and looked ravishing in his pyjamas...

the stage hands were largely drawn from the porters of Covent Garden fruit and vegetable market. A fairly rough bunch, they were, nonetheless, stage struck, and enjoyed taking part in Drury Lane shows – especially Ivor's, which needed far more backstage crew than most because of the frequent scene changes and the various special effects.

They were not paid a great deal by today's standards – another reason for a lack of Novello shows being the vast expense required to stage them properly – but they took a genuine pleasure and pride in their contribution to Ivor's successes, and were famously loyal to him, giving him the nick-name 'The Guv'nor'.

Unlike the rehearsal for *The Rat*, eleven years earlier, when it had seemed as if the show was doomed to disaster, those for *Glamorous Night* went very well, with Ivor's infectious enthusiasm for the piece effortlessly conveying itself to everyone around him.

The opening night, 2 May 1935, had an amazing buzz about it. Even the hardened old stage door keepers hadn't seen anything like the number of bouquets and telegrams that cascaded in to the theatre. Advance bookings were good, but the first night was completely sold out.

It's title, *Glamorous Night*, was a perfect description of that May evening, seventy years ago. This was an era when, despite what the older generation considered to be a lowering of standards since the (First World) War, those who could afford to dressed up to go to the theatre, the men wearing dinner jackets at plays and, often, white tie and tails at the opera or the grander musicals like Ivor's. The women wore dresses by fashionable couturiers like Molyneux (or Captain Molyneux, as Queen Mary referred to him) and as many jewels as they could get away with without being accused of vulgarity.

It was also an age when stars were meant to look like stars, off stage as well as on. This could lead to a certain superficiality – Isabel Jeans, on being offered a part in a new play asked not who the director was, or who her co-stars were, but "Who's doing the dresses?" On the other hand, it was an era when there was a genuine glamour about the West End and the lives of its stars. The fact that so many people lived in what today would be considered unacceptable, grinding, poverty merely made the stars seem to shine all the brighter. It may not have scored highly in terms of morals, but the minks were fabulous.

By the time Ivor made his curtain-call speech (another charming West End tradition that has quietly died) at the end of the evening, it was clear that he had had the greatest personal triumph of his career. The show exceeded the public's wildest expectations, and more than lived up to its title. What is interesting, though, is that for all the glamour, Ivor mixed romance with the latest technology, and had the confidence to open the show, not in a palace, but in a suburban street.

He played a twenty-something (he was now forty-two) television inventor, in a year when television was as high tech and unrelated to everyday life as the wildest shores of genetic engineering are today. The inventor, Anthony Allen, needs a patron. Fed up with the lack of interest in his product in Britain (some things never change) he takes a short holiday to Krasnia, where King Stefan has a mistress, the opera singer Militza Hajos, and a Prime Minister who is plotting against him.

Anthony, being a young man of culture as well as technological ability, decides to visit the opera, where he foils an assassination attempt on Militza – well, this is a musical. She, grateful, offers to fund his television station. Their relationship might have been strictly a business one, had it not been for the fact that Prime Minister Lydyeff insists that she leave the country, as her affair is making the King unpopular.

In fact, she is the King's greatest ally, and demonstrates this by quelling a noisy revolutionary demonstration with a spirited rendition of the Krasnian national anthem – if only Tsar Nicholas II had known more opera singers. As a concession to Lydyeff, she offers to go on a cruise, but insists she will return when things have calmed down.

By a happy coincidence Anthony is travelling on the same ship. Ivor, well aware of the glamour of 1930s liners, made the most of the episode at sea, and even threw in a beautiful stowaway – the American singer, Elisabeth Welch, who had been something of a muse to Cole Porter. As a black singer, her opportunities had been limited in America, but her decision to try her luck in Paris and London worked. Ivor had seen her in *Nymph Errant*, recognised her talent and gave her a chance to further her career at Drury Lane with a lilting, poignant song, 'Shanty Town'.

Maximising the advanced stage technology available at Drury Lane (and the hydraulic lifts that made the effects possible can still be seen during a backstage tour of the theatre) Ivor decided to treat the audience to an on-stage shipwreck, caused by the Prime Minster's agents planting a bomb on board to dispose of Militza. Needless to say, Militza and Anthony reach shore safely – and with not a hair out of place – and come across a gypsy encampment. Militza turns out to have some gypsy blood in her, and the two lovers – for they have, of course, fallen in love – are married in an elaborate ceremony.

This being an Ivor Novello show the gypsies are not poorly or simply clothed, but positively dripping in lace, frills, and exquisite costumes. Their happiness is shattered when word comes that the King's life is in danger. Anthony and Militza hurry back to Krasnia and foil the Prime Minister, who is pointing a gun at King Stefan and threatening to shoot him if he doesn't sign the deed of Abdication that he has prepared.

A shot rings out, but it is the Prime Minister who has been hit, by Anthony, who turns out to be a marksman as well as a strong swimmer. Militza realises that the King needs her, the lovers decided to keep their marriage secret, and she marries the King, who agrees, as a reward for saving his life and looking after Militza, to give Anthony the balance of the money he needs for his television project. The only condition is that the first broadcast must be of Militza, which it duly is, even though it breaks Anthony's heart.

By the time the curtain eventually fell, the first night audience had been treated to songs of a sumptuous richness and romanticism that fully live up to the show's title: 'Fold Your Wings' and 'Shine Through My Dreams' are operetta bordering on opera, and the 'Glamorous Night' waltz sent Mary Ellis' voice soaring up to the balcony – and out though the box office: overnight it became London's sought-after show.

Ivor's PR manager believed that, however brilliant his other first nights, Glamorous Night's was the most exciting. Using a phrase with an unimaginably different meaning several decades later, *the Bystander* was of the opinion that: 'Highbrow authors…may pettishly suggest that the whole thing is punk. It may be so, but it is inspired punk…'

The *Observer* summarised Ivor's appeal better than any of its rivals:

'I lift my hat off to Mr Novello. He can wade through tosh with the straightest face: the tongue never visibly approaches the cheek…'

Ivor's own creed, as far as *Glamorous Night* and its successors were concerned, was straightforward and heartfelt. Speaking to *Women's Pictorial* in April 1950, and paraphrasing several other women's magazine articles over the years, he said:

'I am not a highbrow. I am an entertainer. Empty seats and good opinions mean nothing to me…I am an unrepentant sentimentalist. I have always tried in everything that I have written to appeal first to the heart. Rightly or wrongly I believe that the theatre is primarily a place of make-believe.'

The fact that this was a musical without a happy ending gave it an original and effective edge, though Ivor was taken to task by King George V, whose Jubilee Year this was. Having been to see *Glamorous Night*, he invited Ivor to a garden party at Buckingham Palace, where he asked him to ensure that, in future, he wrote a musical with a happy ending, as *Glamorous Night* had made the Queen cry.

History does not record whether Mam was invited to the garden party along with Ivor: he probably took one of his leading ladies, on the grounds that it would help his public image and provide fewer opportunities for potential embarrassment. George V had already received a shock from Mam when, a few years earlier, he had opened India House in the Aldwych. As his carriage procession passed the Strand Theatre, Mam and her ageing Welsh singers, dressed in full Welsh folk costume, suddenly appeared on the parapet of the flat's roof, and burst into 'God Save the King', to the royal party's astonishment.

Ivor's natural elation was short-lived. Bookings for *Glamorous Night* were the envy of every other show in town, but he found, to his fury, that although the Board of Drury Lane had agreed to stage the show, they had not had all that much confidence in the product, and so had booked a pantomime in for the Christmas season, which meant that, however good the box office receipts or projected profits, *Glamorous Night* would be limited to a run of a few months, and though he might well make a fortune with the show on tour (he did) Ivor would not be able to have a decent run in London.

The Board compounded their bad behaviour with a lack of artistic judgement when Ivor offered them a new musical for when the panto came off. Christopher Hassall was the lyricist, and Leontine Sagan would be director again. The Board thanked Ivor for his trouble but turned him down in favour of a show called, optimistically, *Rise and Shine*. This was a blow, but, like all Ivor's reverses, he followed it with a successful come-back, with his next musical, *Careless Rapture*.

Ivor, impossibly handsome, mid 1930s

CARELESS RAPTURE

It was thanks to the Board at Drury Lane that Ivor had the time, in 1936, to perform *The Happy Hypocrite* at His Majesty's Theatre. When Rise and Shine flopped and folded, Drury Lane were forced to ask him whether he would, after all, consider taking the theatre for his new show, called *Careless Rapture* – after some poetry by Robert Browning:

> That's the wise thrush; he sings each song twice over,
> Lest you should think he never could recapture
> The first fine careless rapture!

Ivor wasn't always so highbrow about the titles of his shows – he was to give them facetious nick-names in due course – *Careless Rapture* became *Careless Rupture*, *Perchance to Dream* was *Perchance to Scream*, while *The Dancing Years* was, in male company, *The Prancing Queers*. After the latter had been running for nearly six years, and in mixed company who would not have appreciated the previous nick-name, he referred to it as *The Advancing Years*.

Careless Rapture is particularly interesting in that, unlike *Glamorous Night*, and contrary to his general reputation, the show is not set in a Ruritanian never-never land, nor are there members of a Royal Family involved. True, there is an aristocrat, and glamorous women, but the show is, essentially a very chic, very Art Deco piece, with a taste for the all white decor made fashionable by Syrie Maugham and associated, today, with 1920s and 1930s smart society.

The opening, in a fashionable beauty parlour, pokes fun at

Love finally triumphs in Careless Rapture, 1936

the rich and would-be elegant, while simultaneously dazzling the audience with the set, clothes and actresses that Ivor and Leontine Sagan had assembled. This time his leading lady was not Mary Ellis, but another American star, Dorothy Dickson, one of the most glamorous (a word one cannot help repeating in

connection with the Novello circle) actresses of her generation, whose almost equally beautiful daughter, Dorothy Hyson was to marry Sir Anthony Quayle, a remarkably fine stage actor who is, unfortunately, primarily remembered for a handful of war films.

The plot was, in a sense, more improbable than that of *Glamorous Night*. Ivor played another twenty-something (he was

147

now forty-three), Michael, who is an illegitimate member of an aristocratic family. His wicked half brother, Sir Rodney, hates him, and insists on enforcing the terms of the allowance the family pay Michael – that he is only allowed to visit England for a short time or he forfeits his money.

Michael meets and falls in love with a singer, Penny (Dorothy Dickson) who is giving a farewell concert – as she is about to marry Sir Rodney! He follows her about, including to a singing lesson, where her voice is being exercised by Madame Simonetti (Olive Gilbert). The singing lesson gave Ivor his only official (see *Perchance to Dream*) chance to sing – mercifully briefly – on stage.

Since his voice broke, his career as a singer had been over, but he never quite gave up hope that he might make a comeback. Preparing for the role in *Careless Rapture* involved singing scales in a rehearsal room in Covent Garden: the children who lived nearby and in painful earshot made such a pointed racket when they heard him at his exercises that he finally took the hint. An exchange about the quality of his voice that takes place in this scene was, given his war-time disaster, rather ironic.

Michael tells Penny he feels his future is in opera – she suggests jail to be more likely, to which he ripostes; "No, opera. The food's better."

Other songs are the operatic 'Love Made The Song I Sing To You', and the very jazzy 'Wait For Me', and the operetta-style 'Music in May.'

Having fallen in love, Michael and Penny run off to the funfair on Hampstead Heath where they are tracked down by Sir Rodney, who cuts off Michael's inheritance.

We next find Penny in China, in a local production of the show, *The Rose Girl*, that made her famous. Michael turns up in disguise – in full Chinese costume – but is discovered by Sir Rodney. An earthquake ("My maid says it's earthquake weather" announces Dorothy Dickson, helpfully, just before the city collapses into rubble) destroys the buildings around them (more work for the Drury Lane special effects team) and, to compound their problems, they are then kidnapped by Chinese bandits. It had been the real-life kidnapping of

148

an Englishwoman that gave Ivor the original inspiration for the show.

Eventually Penny and Michael escape, leaving the wicked Sir Rodney in the bandits' clutches. Returning to civilisation, they are married in an all-white wedding ceremony at a temple and live happily ever after. George V, who died in the January of that year, would have been delighted, as the theatre critic of Variety certainly was, describing *Careless Rapture* as: 'The best of its kind ever conceived.'

Ivor modelling a more casual look in a stage door café

CREST OF THE WAVE & THE DANCING YEARS

Few people thought that Ivor would be able to bring off a hat-trick at Drury Lane, but he did, with *Crest of the Wave*, which opened on 1 September 1937, and seemed to prove that Ivor's career was on one too.

The plot involved another spectacular disaster; this time a train crash, and, inspired perhaps by his make-up in *The Happy Hypocrite*, Ivor played not only the hero – Don Gantry – but the villain – Otto Fresch.

The inspiration for *Crest of the Wave* came, like his previous two shows, from real life: in this case it was the young aristocrat, Brook Warwick, who went to Hollywood and was believed to be destined for stardom. The stardom failed to materialise, and Ivor's own memories of Hollywood were not very satisfying ones, but given the prevalence of American movies over British films – and this was, after all, the Golden Age of Hollywood – he felt that having the movies in the plot would be a crowd-pleaser.

The scenery was certainly varied – from a decrepit Stately Home to the film studios of California; the humour was, if anything, better than in the earlier musicals; Ivor was at his most elegant – as yet another twenty-something, though by now aged forty-four; there was yet another ocean-going liner (which was transformed, at one point, into a full-scale battleship) as well as the smoke and noise of the train crash; but *Crest of the Wave* was somehow less satisfying an experience than *Glamorous Night* or *Careless Rapture*.

Of the dozen or so songs, one of the most charming was a duet, 'Why Isn't It You', where a couple who get on well and should be lovers find that there simply isn't the sexual spark between them that is essential if they are to upgrade friendship to romance. 'If You Only Knew' is also attractive, but fairly lightweight – as one could say of the show as a whole.

The only song from *Crest of the Wave* that has had any sort of shelf-life is 'Rose of England', a rousingly patriotic number sung by the ghosts of dead medieval knights who used to sally forth from the stately home of the Gantry family to fight England's foes in ages past. Frequently played as incidental music at ceremonial occasions, like Trooping the Colour or Remembrance Sunday at the Cenotaph in Whitehall, if one didn't know who the tune was by, one would guess it was by Elgar. It has all the stateliness of Land of Hope and Glory without any of the brashness or swagger, and would make an excellent English National Anthem as and when the United Kingdom is split into its constituent parts. It would be a particularly applicable National Anthem when, as now, we have a female sovereign, and for the next few decades the song's title will continue to conjure up images of Princess Diana, commemorated by Sir Elton John as 'England's rose'.

Crest of the Wave ran for less than a year and though the enormous size of the Theatre Royal, Drury Lane, meant that that was equivalent to a two-year run at any other London theatre, it had proved that Ivor could write three crowd-pullers in a row, but it was not the ideal show for him to be remembered by. If anything, he had overwhelmed his audience rather than charmed it, as the *Observer* confessed: 'One staggers out sated and a trifle stunned, observing, with a bloated species of relief, as one does at the end of a long Christmas dinner with the family, that this occasion is over for another year.'

Having, therefore, had two relatively disappointing shows in a row, *Crest of the Wave* and *Henry V*, Ivor he felt he had to prove to his critics, and rivals, that he was still the major force in the West End. This time, not even the Luftwaffe could stop him – though they did make him change theatres – and on 23 March, 1939, he had his last Drury Lane first night, this time in a show called *The Dancing Years*.

Once again, Ivor based a show on a real event. While on holiday in Venice, he had been appalled when a friend told him that he had recently been in Vienna, and had found (Austria having become

152

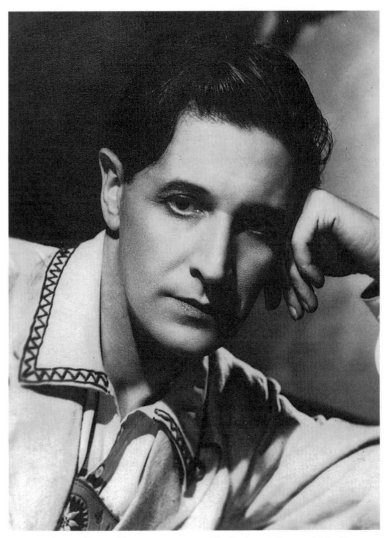

Ivor at 46, wondering if he can get away with playing a 23 year old in The Dancing Years, *1939*

part of the Third Reich in 1938) that the Nazis had banned the sale of records of music by Jewish composers.

Ivor, of course, was not Jewish, though one theatre critic had been sent a hate letter asking why he had recently praised a show by that 'little Jew, Novello'. Presumably the ghastly correspondent had been short-sighted as well as bigoted, for Ivor's dark hair and Mediterranean complexion made him come across, if anything, as

Italian. As, too, did his name, which he officially adopted by deed poll in 1927, signing David Ivor Davies into the dusty recesses of family history.

Ivor's sympathy for the plight of the Jews was a humanitarian one rather than a family matter, therefore, and in his case it was humanitarian in a particular way. He felt horror for the treatment of a fellow artist, and tried to picture himself in a similar situation. To that degree, his sympathy was, as with most of his interests, essentially a personal (and critics might say selfish) one. He was not concerned with the ebb and flow of history, still less with day to day politics, but continental politics were beginning to affect the lives and work of artists – in the broadest sense of the word – to an unprecedented degree.

Ivor, unlike his contemporaries – who are presented as far more serious and worthwhile artists than he could ever have been with his looks, escapist plots and romantic music – Ivor, and Ivor alone, was to express his outrage, to the horror of his producer and the dismay of the government, by addressing the behaviour of the Nazis on the West End stage, albeit in a musical.

The political, commentary, it is true, is reserved for the end of the play, and even then Ivor had to fight Tom Arnold, his producer, who would have been much happier losing it altogether. The rest of the action can be taken, simply, as a charming, and entirely mainstream, musical. It is the epilogue that provides the kick.

Essentially, *The Dancing Years* tells the story of a young Jewish Austrian composer, Rudi Kleber. When the Drury Lane audience first saw him, on 23 March 1939, Rudi was meant to be in his early twenties – Ivor was now forty-six. Amazingly, he could still carry it off when on stage, with the benefit of appropriate make-up and lighting, together with the fact that he still had remarkably good (and firm) skin in any case. At that point he did not need to dye his hair, though he had to later, until he played a character his own age in *King's Rhapsody*, in 1949. He did, however, look his age when seen in close up, on camera, which is why he didn't appear in the 1937 film of *Glamorous Night*.

He never had plastic surgery himself, though he toyed with the idea when he was in his fifties, but was fascinated by its potential for 'tidying up' the faces of those with less perfect profiles than himself. He arranged a 'nose job' for his old friend and loyal personal secretary, Lloyd Williams ('Lloydy'), and gave one to Vanessa Lee, to improve her looks prior to *King's Rhapsody*.

No little trims were needed by his leading lady in *The Dancing Years*, Mary Ellis, who returned to Drury Lane to play another opera singer, this time called Maria Ziegler, the toast of pre-First World War Vienna. Where a particular theme worked in one of his shows, Ivor often re-used it in a later one, rather as some of the tunes first performed on stage in the 1930s had been written by him in the 1910s.

Sometimes critics thought that they had been written even earlier, and by other people. Like many famous composers he was sometimes (though never directly) accused of plagiarism. While it is certainly true that he was heavily influenced by Puccini and Lehàr – and loved Wagner – his tunes are his own, though there may have been the occasional unconscious 'borrowing' from the music of his childhood. In one of the many stories told about Lilian Braithwaite, she was at an Ivor Novello musical with a friend. As the orchestra got into their stride with his newest 'big tune', the friend turned to Lilian and said: "Oh, naughty Ivor! That's an old Welsh hymn!" To which Lilian shot back: "Which is more than can be said for the composer!"

Back in *The Dancing Years*... Rudi cannot afford to pay his hotel bill, and he may have to sell his piano, in which case he will be ruined. A twelve-year old girl, Grete (played by Roma Beaumont) whose aunt is the hotel's housekeeper, is in love with Rudi, but he, being older, treats her like an older brother, to her annoyance. Roma had been 'discovered' by Tom Arnold when she joined the touring production of *Crest of the Wave*. He had persuaded Ivor to see her. Impressed, Ivor had, typically, told her that he would make her a star – which he did, not just through the role of Grete but by leading her forward by the hand on the first night of *The Dancing Years* and telling the audience how talented he thought she was. He may have had a fellow feeling for her, as well, in that she looked so much younger than she was (she was twenty when *The Dancing Years* opened). During the War she grew tired of playing Grete, and asked Ivor if he could find something else for her. He did. He backed a production, in which she had the starring role – as *Alice in Wonderland*!

While talking to Grete about his money worries, Rudi is saved from ruin by the arrival of a group of young officers and their girlfriends. The gallant young soldiers sing 'Uniform', a celebration of the variety of dashing costumes available to aristocratic young men under the Hapsburgs. Rudi performs his songs to them, for money, and is heard by Maria, who happens, conveniently, to be passing by. She purchases a song, becomes his patroness and they fall in love. Having fallen for Rudi she ditches her previous lover, Prince Charles Metterling.

Rudi becomes a successful composer, and one scene has him conducting his opera at the Vienna Opera House. This was the nearest Ivor came to realising his mother's ambition for him to conduct his own, at Covent Garden. Mam died during the long wartime run of *The Dancing Years*, in 1943. She had continued to turn up to Ivor's first nights, beaming with goodwill and brandy, a stout, ruddy faced old girl swathed in furs and jewels provided by Ivor, who kept a permanent room for her at Redroofs.

By the end of her life she had finally, thanks to old age, calmed down a little, which saved him from having to bail her out of financial catastrophes, with all the tears and tantrums that such efforts inevitably produced. Her last, and most dramatic adventure had been in 1938, when she had suddenly upped and left with the remnants of her Welsh Grandmothers Choir, determined to give a series of continental concerts from the Netherlands to Nuremburg, at the heart of Nazi Germany, where she would sing to Hitler and persuade him of the necessity of peace. Fortunately for all concerned (especially Hitler) she got no further than the first stage of her odyssey, which ended with a telegram to Ivor, claiming that everything was going swimmingly and would he please send her £4000 immediately. He did so, but it was the cause of their last and loudest row, with her insisting that things were bound to improve – despite the fact that her empty concerts had been cancelled.

Mam, as ever, had the last word. When war was finally declared, the following September, she looked at Ivor and said: 'You see? If you'd let me go to Germany...' When Ivor

Mary Elllis, the singer with a fringe on top...

wrote the foreword to her autobiography, published in 1940, he admitted that he hadn't actually read the book. The truth was that he couldn't bear to, as he knew he was likely to be upset by the inevitable discrepancies between Mam's recollections of events and the facts. Nevertheless he continued to be the perfect son to her, aware that she had, in her time, been a justly famous music teacher, and that he owed his hot-house musical education, and the vital introductions and personal contacts of his adolescence, to her.

After the opera scene – Mam's favourite – with its appropriately dramatic love song, 'My Life Belongs To You', sung by Dunstan Hart, *The Dancing Years* continues with Maria and Rudi living together and planning a music festival. It is now several years since their meeting, and Maria is desperate for a child, but Rudi won't marry her, and she will be ruined if she becomes pregnant before getting married.

Rudi tries to reassure Maria that he still loves her, despite the 'shadow' that lies between them, and in one of the most popular moments in the show he produces a new song that he has written specially for her – "Oh, Rudi, it's dedicated to me!" "They're all dedicated to you." – which he plays on the piano, talking her through the lyrics, which she then sings. Thanks to a cast recording, we can hear her, too. The song, 'My Dearest Dear' remains the most touching of all Ivor's love songs.

The temporary reprieve it earns Rudi is soon lost, however. Grete, the girl with the crush on Rudi, has been sent away to drama school in England and now returns as a young musical star in her own right. Ivor was very fond of Roma Beaumont, and gave her/Grete a delightful song and dance number, 'Primrose' which was an affectionate tribute to the Edwardian songs of his youth. The lyrics, and the tone of the music, are not far removed from 'How Much is That Doggy in the Window', but Roma's charm, and the skill with which she executed the dance, stopped the show every night. The *Daily Sketch* thought 'Mr Novello's best achievement of all this lovely, colourful production is his discovery of Roma Beaumont, in whom unquestionably a star is born.'

Before going to England, Grete made Rudi promise that when she has grown up, he will ask her to marry him. She has no intention of holding him to his proposal, but at least he will have been the first man ever to ask her, and she will be the first girl he asks. This is why Rudi, a man of great honour, will not ask Maria to marry him, and he feels he cannot break his promise of secrecy to Grete to explain things to Maria.

When Grete returns, she reminds Rudi of his promise, he goes through the motions of asking her – and is heard, on the staircase behind him, by Maria, who only hears him ask the question – none of the explanatory banter that precedes it. Desperately hurt Maria runs off. When she returns, Rudi, who had been frantic with worry, explains everything, but it is all, tragically, too late. In her anguish she has married the one man who had always loved her – Prince Charles Metterling.

The action then moves forwards to after the War, and subsequent Revolution. It is now the 1920s and we hear a syncopated version of 'My Dearest Dear' being played in the background as Maria meets Rudi in a café, and asks him to see her again, out of town. When Rudi arrives at their rendezvous, Maria shows him her son. In the course of their conversation, Rudi realises that the boy is his, not Prince Charles'. This, and the fact that Maria clearly still loves him, is unbearably poignant. It is also consistent with the theme than ran through his first musical, *Glamorous Night* – that duty comes before love.

Rudi knows that there are storm clouds on the horizon. The warning that he gives Maria in the café scene had a contemporary resonance for *The Dancing Years'* audience in the run-up to, and during the long years of, the Second World War:

'We are going to see great changes I know…There's so much unrest and unhappiness in the world – we shall almost forget to smile and make music – but we shan't quite forget, and some day we'll wake up from an evil dream and forget to hate, and the world will smile again and the sweetness of music and friendliness will once more be important…'

The final scene of *The Dancing Years* shows Rudi in prison, where the Nazis have been trying to break his spirit, after arresting him for helping Jews escape from Austria. There is the equivalent of a good cop and a bad cop, whose conversation gives the audience the background information it needs – for example, that Rudi's music has been banned.

Just as things look very bleak for him, Maria, Princess Metterling, arrives with an order from her husband who is a senior figure in the new regime – the soldiers refer to him as 'His Excellency'. Rudi is, temporarily, saved, but he tells Maria that he will continue his work against the regime, strengthened by the knowledge of the rightness of his cause, and secure in the knowledge of her love.

She reassures him that, even if he is killed, his music, to which a generation danced, will live on.

After this moving speech the scene fades from the prison to the open stage, where scores of couples gradually appear, until the whole theatre seems full of them and then, from the back of the stage, Rudi and Maria appear, waltzing together towards the audience, as the curtain falls.

This final scene may sound rather hackneyed, but the visual and emotional impact, especially after the harrowing prison scene, worked very well. This is an important point with Ivor's plays and, even more, his musicals. He had a highly accurate instinct for what would work in a theatre, for his audiences. Tastes change, and what worked with the public in the 1920s, 30s and 40s would not necessarily work now, but Ivor was writing for the present, not for posterity.

Many times friends would read his scripts, and feared the worse, only to be as impressed as everyone else with the finished product. Listening to a recording of *The Dancing Years* proves the point. Words that limp across a page come alive when spoken in the theatre. Add to that Ivor's stage presence, which even his critics admitted he had, and the sets, costumes and other characters on stage, the power of his music and the dazzling dance numbers, and one can see why he was so popular.

The Dancing Years more than made up for the deficiencies of *Crest of the Wave,* but when war was declared in September, the prospect of a mass bombing campaign led to the London theatres being temporarily closed. As with *Glamorous Night,* it looked as if forces beyond Ivor's immediate control were going to wreck the prospect of a decent London run with a new musical, but in a topical spirit of defiance he decided instead to take it on tour. While waiting for this to be organised he wrote and appeared in *Ladies Into Action* (originally called *Second Helping*), at the Lyric in April 1940. It co-starred Isabel Jeans and Lilli Palmer.

Far from being closed by the Second World War, *The Dancing Years* lasted as long as it did, running from 1939 to 1945. Ivor took it on tour through the country, and then returned for a London run at the Adelphi Theatre in the Strand, Drury Lane having been taken over for the duration of hostilities by the

160

Ivor, Isabel Jeans and Dorothy Dickson advertising Second Helping (later called Ladies Into Action, with Lilli Palmer replacing Miss Dickson)

armed forces entertainment service, ENSA, known to the troops as 'Every Night Something Awful.'

Noël Coward later decried Ivor's war effort, writing in his diary the year after hostilities ceased, that : 'He told me how he evaded fire-watching and flew to the shelter whenever danger threatened.'

Whatever Noël's reservations, and Ivor's attitude to air raids, his achievement in carrying on with the show in wartime London is remarkable, given not only the threat of bombs but the difficulties with members of cast being called up to fight. Ivor's tours of *The Dancing Years*, with all the wartime shortages and transport problems, show his commitment to theatre and the underlying determination beneath his outwardly romantic and other-worldly manner.

He needed all of this toughness towards the end of the run, when he was sentenced to a month in prison for fuel rationing offences. This episode, which reflected badly on the British justice system, came about through a combination of official pettiness, Ivor's refusal to do without the comforts he had been used to since he first became wealthy in 1914, and the infatuation of one of his fans.

The number and enthusiasm of Ivor's female fans has already been commented on. One of them, known as Grace Walton but whose real name was Dora Constable (an unfortunate surname, as it turned out), was in Ivor's dressing room towards the end of 1942, and heard him say that as the relevant ministry had turned down his application for a special licence so he could drive to Redroofs from London in the Rolls after the Saturday evening show, he might as well give it away.

Grace Walton came up with what seemed the perfect idea. She worked for a company in Reading: not all that far from Redroofs, which was near Maidenhead. Why not let her transfer the Rolls to her company, then the company could arrange for Ivor to be given a lift in what had been his car. If he was going to get rid of it anyway, this would be a perfect solution to the problem, as the ministry would be bound to issue a licence once the car was being used by an industrial company (and therefore the war effort) rather than Ivor's personal comfort.

Ivor, delighted, agreed at once, but with the proviso that he would continue to pay the salary of his chauffeur, Morgan, who had worked loyally for him for many years. Unfortunately, he didn't say anything about the arrangement to his solicitor – possibly because he didn't want any quibbling to jeopardise what seemed a perfect arrangement.

After nearly a year, however, it turned out to be far from

Mary Ellis has a Jessie Matthews moment...

perfect. Grace Walton was really Dora Constable, she was just a clerk who had no authority to make the deal with Ivor, and her employers wrote to Ivor to say that they had discovered this highly irregular 'arrangement'.

Annoyed, but not expecting any trouble, Ivor thought he should contact the authorities to inform them of the situation. To his horror he found that he was to be made a public example of, and was summonsed to appear at Bow Street Magistrates Court,

Olive Gilbert, one of Ivor's closest friends, whose support was crucial during his trial

a short walk from his flat in the Aldwych, to face a charge of conspiracy to break the law.

The trial took place on 24 April 1944, under a judge who was a heavy sentencer with a marked dislike for the acting profession, and for gay men in particular. The odds were against Ivor. He was, however, his own worst enemy in that his performance in court was the worse of his life, with him appearing to simply blame Dora Constable for everything, and refusing to take any blame himself.

To 'hide behind a woman' was at best ungallant and at worst – in the judge's eyes – unmanly and contemptible. The fact that she was responsible for the whole mess was irrelevant. The crucial accusation was not that Ivor had broken the law – that was not in dispute – but that he had conspired to do so. The fact that he had continued to pay Morgan's salary was seen, not as the generous gesture of a kindly employer, but damning evidence that the whole 'arrangement' about the car was a sham, and planned as such by Ivor as Miss Walton/Constable, so Ivor could circumvent the regulations, putting his personal luxury above the law, at a time when many had been bombed out of their homes, let alone deprived of their Rolls Royces over the week-end.

The fact that Ivor was, in terms of everyday life, impractical, that he was used to a loyal and loving staff smoothing every path in life for him – despite the savage rationing rules, constant presents of food from friends and admirers meant that his dressing room at the Adelphi resembled the Food Hall at Fortnum and Mason's – counted for nothing in the courtroom, or merely confirmed the judge's belief that Ivor thought the real world shouldn't impinge on his theatrical one. This, the judge decided, was one occasion on which it would.

Dora Constable was fined, and sent on her way, though her real punishment was the banishment from Ivor's charmed circle. The judge told Ivor that a fine would indeed be the usual punishment, but that as – "to a man like you" – this would be a negligible inconvenience, he was sentenced to two months in prison.

Ivor's lawyer issued an immediate appeal and he was freed on bail. MacQueen Pope, his PR manager, thought he should have pleaded guilty (which he technically was), claimed that he had not realised that he was committing an offence, that he had behaved foolishly and ignorantly rather than criminally, and thrown himself on the court's mercy. This advice was ignored, and a not guilty plea was entered for the appeal case, which was heard on 16 May.

Caught in a waking nightmare, he again performed badly in court. The verdict was upheld, and although the sentence was halved to four weeks, he was still sent to prison – to Wormwood Scrubs.

Many of his friends thought the prison sentence broke his health, if not his spirit, and that it was responsible for his early death. This is to exaggerate the impact the sentence had on him. At the time, he was distraught, and was only saved from a nervous breakdown thanks to the kindness of the prison chaplain, another Welshman, who arranged for him to be spared normal duties, and put him in charge of the prison choir. Although it was an enormous humiliation, the worse thing about the sentence was having to spend so much time locked up, alone.

All through his life he had been used to being surrounded by people, the centre not just of attention but affection. He had his servants, his friends, his fellow actors and actresses, his fans, his lovers. He was the centre of a loyal circle wherever he went, and was used to the best of everything. He did not spend money ostentatiously (with the possible exception of having his initials emblazoned on the doors of the Rolls) but he spent a great deal in order to maintain his two households in England and, later, his home in Jamaica.

The contrast between this and a prison cell was unbearable. He later wrote that he had sometimes wondered whether a disaster that threw him on his own devices would reveal depths of character or profounder thoughts, but that, when it happened, he nearly went mad with boredom and loneliness, as well as self-pity.

Having served his time he was released shortly after midnight, in order to avoid the inevitable attentions of the press. After a short period spent recuperating he returned to the Adelphi theatre and *The Dancing Years*. In prison he had confided to the chaplain that he wanted to retire from public life. He had enough money never to have to work again. But his work was his life, and after his release, despite being unsure of the public's reaction, he decided to return to the stage.

He was, understandably, nervous as he walked (for once – normally he took the Rolls but that would have been tactless, to say the least) to the stage door of the Adelphi, in Maiden Lane. Recognised by some passers-by, he was given a few words of encouragement that gave a disproportionate boost to his morale. Once back in the theatre he felt his strength return, but the critical

Roma Beaumont, who co-starred in The Dancing Years and Perchance To Dream

moment would come when he appeared on stage. What would happen? Silence? Jeers? Cat-calls about the rich?

The cast and his whole entourage were equally nervous, and the wings were packed with people as Ivor, playing Rudi Kleber, appeared on stage. As soon as they saw him the audience burst into the loudest cheers and applause that any of those on stage or in the wings could ever remember. The ovation last for several minutes before Ivor was able to calm them down and carry on with the show.

The authorities' decision to make an example of him had backfired terribly. The vindictiveness of the sentence, contrasted with the fact that Ivor inspired a protective and personal affection from friends and public alike that was – and remains – unrivalled by any other performer, had led to a sense of public outrage. Sir Edward Marsh had gone directly to Winston Churchill, who agreed that the sentence was a travesty, but insisted that there was nothing, as Prime Minister, that he could do.

Far from suffering social ostracism and personal ruin, Ivor was seen as a martyr. Some commentators attributed the failure of his musical, *Arc de Triomphe* (starring Mary Ellis, featuring Elisabeth Welch, set in Paris and opening at the Phoenix Theatre on 9 November 1943) to the bad publicity caused by the trial, whose timing coincided with that of the musical's demise. The truth was that *Arc de Triomphe* was not one of his best shows, that the twin themes of Thwarted Love and France Will Rise Again were both done far more effectively in the Bogart/Bergman film *Casablanca*, that the Germans' new flying bombs put off audiences and, worst of all, this was an Ivor Novello musical in which Ivor Novello did not appear.

The only other flop that Ivor had in this period was a play, *Breakaway*, also known as *Break For Romance*, about a chain-store owning millionairess who decides to leave the world of commerce behind her and travel to Venice. A well-written piece which Ivor clearly thought would remind audiences of happier times and sunnier places (the Venetian scenes take part in a Princess' Palazzo), it opened for a short run at the Theatre Royal, Windsor, before disappearing into theatre archives – today even most Novello fans are unaware that it ever existed. Another discarded play is *Blood Royal*, which is a prototype for his last major musical, *King's Rhapsody*, in that it deals with worldly Princes living in Paris, exotic mistresses and the political intrigues of mythical Balkan kingdoms. It was discovered, in the early 1990s, in the trunks of Novello material that is kept at Samuel French, who act for Ivor's estate, and publish the scripts of his musicals.

Just as it is a myth that the prison sentence killed *Arc de Triomphe*, so it is a myth that Ivor went to an early grave because of his month in jail. He managed a joke as he left Wormwood Scrubs; on the very rare occasions he ever spoke about the experience he deflected expressions of sympathy with humour; he donated a piano to the prison chapel and arranged for occasional concerts by singers from West End shows to alleviate the prison boredom that he had found so intolerable – though, not unnaturally, he never performed at these himself.

What paved the way to his death at fifty-eight was a combination of his sixty-a-day cigarette habit, a weak chest and several terrible winters, the effects of the infamous London smog, now relegated to history, which killed hundreds of people every year, and, specifically, a heart attack, which he was genetically susceptible to – his father, also a heavy smoker, had died of one twenty years before.

His release from prison took place at about the time of the D Day landings and as soon as he was able, he crossed the Channel to Normandy, to provide entertainment for the troops. He took a play, *Love From A Stranger*, to France, where he performed close to the front line, his own lines sometimes having to be shouted above the background roar of an endless stream of warplanes.

After the show, which he performed with a cast that included Diana Wynyard and Margaret Rutherford, he gave concerts on a battered piano, always starting with his hit from the previous war, 'Keep the Home Fires Burning'. It was at one such performance that he gave the first public airing to 'We'll Gather Lilacs', which was to be the hit number of his next musical, *Perchance to Dream*.

Ivor prepares for some 'Highwayman Love' in Perchance to Dream, 1945

PERCHANCE TO DREAM

Perchance to Dream opened at the London Hippodrome on 21 April 1945, with regular Novello players like Bobbie Andrews, Roma Beaumont, Muriel Barron (who had taken over from Mary Ellis in *The Dancing Years* while Miss Ellis took on war work in hospitals), Olive Gilbert – and Margaret Rutherford, as Lady Charlotte Fayre.

Ivor thought very highly of Margaret Rutherford as an actress, but liked her principally for her eccentric and endearing personality. On one occasion she was invited, along with a handful of other women, to a basically male party at the flat in the Aldwych. As she took in the drawing room packed with beautiful young actors and older grandees like Edward Marsh, she excitedly said to her host: "Oh, Ivor! So many lovely people! Enchanting! It's...it's like fairyland!" Needless to say this became a catch-phrase for Ivor's friends.

The plot of *Perchance to Dream* is one of love surviving the centuries. Set in a beautiful old English house, Huntersmoon, it tells of a love story over three generations – in effect, this is a musical about re-incarnation – with love only working out the third time around. As a result Ivor (and Roma Beaumont and Muriel Barron) had three roles to perform; a challenge he enjoyed.

The best known song is 'We'll Gather Lilacs', which left not a dry eye in the house, and is one of the most romantic tunes written in any musical – British or American. It's theme of looking forward to returning home, and the simple pleasures of the English countryside, had a powerful emotional appeal to a nation battered by years of war. Christopher Hassall had been called up for National Service, so Ivor wrote the lyrics, which fit the mood of the music perfectly:

We'll gather lilacs in the Spring again
And walk together down an English lane
Until our hearts have learned to sing again
When you are home once more.

And in the evening by the firelight's glow
You'll hold me close and never let me go
Your eyes will tell me all I want to know
When you are home once more.

Written over sixty years ago, the song still has an emotional power on audiences. When played during a talk on British theatre to a group of American tourists, most of whom had never heard of Ivor, they, like British audiences who are more conditioned to his music, are clearly moved by it – there is that utter silence, when the song is finished, that only comes when an audience has been completely captured by a mood that words or music have created.

'We'll Gather Lilacs' is often sung solo, or as a duet for a man and a woman – Anne Ziegler and Webster Booth were particularly well-suited to it – but Ivor wrote it as a Victorian song, to be sung by two women: Muriel Barron and Olive Gilbert. Olive Gilbert made the song her party piece for years afterwards, but when I went to visit Muriel Barron at Denville Hall in the late 1990s, a matter of weeks before she died, I made the mistake of mentioning Olive's name in connection with the song. 'Ivor wrote it for me!' this otherwise entirely sweet (and still alert, despite being crippled with arthritis) tiny old lady asserted over lunch, half a century after she and Olive had first sung it together.

Of the other songs in the show, 'Highwayman Love' is perhaps the best, and the Regency setting gave Ivor a chance to wear suitably romantic clothes. *Perchance to Dream*'s popularity was a mixture of the usual Novello romanticism tempered by a gentleness, and nostalgia, that were entirely English and were perfectly suited for the time in which he wrote and performed it.

After a couple of years, Ivor decided to get some much needed sunshine, and he arranged to take *Perchance to Dream* on a tour of

Olive Gilbert, Gordon Duttson, Ivor Novello and Bobbie Andrews in South Africa with Perchance to Dream

South Africa. Margaret Rutherford had left to further her film career, so her part was taken by Zena Dare, while Muriel Barron was replaced with Vanessa Lee, whose break into the big time came in a classic – almost a Hollywood – manner.

She had been working as the understudy to Jessica James, who was playing Maria in *The Dancing Years* at the London Casino (now the Prince Edward Theatre) in Old Compton Street, Soho.

One day Miss James was suffering from a throat infection, but was determined to carry on. She continued acting while, from the wings, Vanessa Lee provided the singing voice. Ivor was called over to the theatre for the unusual event, and was so taken with Vanessa's voice that he promised her a major role in his next production.

As a half-way house he was able to offer her the South African tour of his current show, though he insisted that her name – Ruby Moule – be changed to one more appropriate for a Novello star. Still claiming to have been responsible for Vivien Leigh's stage name, he suggested that as he had brought her good luck, he would use the same initials for young Ruby, and, indeed, the same surname as Vivien, but with a different spelling. By a bizarre coincidence, the same name, Vanessa, that he had chosen (and the two alternatives) had been thought of, independently, by Ruby herself. With a changed name and a nose job she was now ready to become a fully-fledged star, possessed of a pure and soaring voice that was, in its way, as good as that of Mary Ellis.

Vivien Leigh met Ivor and the company of *Perchance to Dream* in South Africa, coming round backstage after the show with Laurence Olivier. One of the many charming things about Ivor was the way that, despite his wealth and fame, he remained as star-struck at fifty as he had been at fifteen. He would always want to know if any celebrities were in the audience, and have them brought round to his dressing room in the interval. Past professional spats could be smoothed over as well, and any ill-feeling over *The Lodger* was to be forgotten and forgiven when Alfred Hitchcock and his family called round to Ivor's dressing room during the run of *King's Rhapsody*. When Ivor invited other stars into his dressing room, he was genuinely thrilled to see them, and that they had chosen to come to see him on stage: there was none of the false emotion and pretend affection that are rife in the theatre. That is not to say that he could not use fake enthusiasm when necessary. He had a highly effective way for dealing with potential critics, especially Noël Coward, who rarely expressed unalloyed praise for anything Ivor did, even to his face. When such a person appeared, dutifully, at Ivor's dressing room door, he pre-empted any of their potentially unflattering comments by beaming at them and saying, before they could even open their mouths: 'I just knew you'd love it, duckie.'

When he could not pre-empt criticism he simply ignored it. Any one daring to make suggestions for improvements to his shows, or his performances within them – and some people were sufficiently egotistic and tactless to do so – were responded to with a smile and the comment:"Thank you, duckie, for your fascinating suggestion." This normally did the trick, without a display of temper, but members of the Musician's Union could be more intransigent.

Ivor was made aware that his habit of singing along, impromptu, to his piano playing during *Perchance to Dream* irritated the members of the orchestra. His response, through clenched teeth, was that if, after thirty years of composing, and over ten years of keeping half the West End employed in vast musicals with huge casts, the orchestra whose salary he was paying begrudged him the little indulgence of singing, quietly, while he played one of his own songs in one of his own shows, they could gently go and ***** themselves.

Despite the undoubted success of *Perchance to Dream*, there was a feeling that American shows, like *Oklahoma!* represented the future direction for musical theatre. This might have dispirited another man, but Ivor was determined, as always, to fight back: he would give them Ruritania with knobs on. The result was to be the best of all his shows, *King's Rhapsody*.

Ivor growing old gracefully

FINAL CURTAIN: KING'S RHAPSODY AND GAY'S THE WORD

Not only is *King's Rhapsody* Ivor's finest work of art, it has a plot which is unnervingly close to the public's view of the Prince Charles/Princess Diana relationship, which would make it a gift for any impresario wanting publicity for a revival. The ideal time for this would have been shortly after the *Panorama* interview in 1995, but her death, though removing some of the topicality, adds an extra layer of tragedy.

The plot has the middle-aged heir to the throne of Murania, Prince Nikki, living in Paris with his mistress, an opera singer (another staple of a Novello show) who happens, for once, to be as old as Ivor's character. Ivor, at last, had written himself a role than was closer to his own age (Nikki is in his early forties, while Ivor was fifty-six), and which enabled him to show his greying hair as is really looked – although being Ivor he had the great good fortune to have replaced his lost youthful beauty with an extraordinarily distinguished and handsome appearance that renewed his fan base from yet another generation of women.

Nikki's mistress, Marta Karillos (as in *Glamorous Night* and *The Dancing Years*, his heroine's name began with an M) was played by the Edwardian musical star and pin-up girl Phyllis Dare. This must have led to a certain about of sibling rivalry as her sister, Zena, also appeared in *King's Rhaspody*, as Nikki's mother! She had played Ivor's mother in *Proscenium* in the 1930s, so her casting in this role (for which her regal looks and bearing made her ideal) was one of many ways in which Ivor deliberately used tried and tested formulae.

Nikki, then, is living in Paris. Queen Elena, the Queen Mother

(Zena Dare) arrives, incognito, to tell him that his father has died, so he is now King. The dialogue between mother and son is witty and quick, reminding audiences of Ivor's skill as a comic writer as well as a composer. She tells Prime Minister Vanescu (Bobbie Andrews) whom he has brought with her, to kneel to his new monarch;

> *Nikki:* Kneel? Monarch? Good God, is the old swine dead?
> *Elena:* I will not have your father called old.
> [There is an exchange of vitriol, with Nikki stung to counter-threat his mother:]
> *Nikki:* Any interference from you ...and I shall have you killed.
> *Elena:* Ah, that's my boy talking.
> *Nikki:* By the way, did my father die a natural death?
> *Elena:* But of course. My own doctor looked after him.

Had we not already had Vanessa Lee singing her heart out as a frigid Snow Princess from Norseland – a kingdom near Murania – we might think we were in a cross between *I, Claudius* and *The Lion in Winter* rather than a Ruritanian musical.

Ivor had lots of tunes to get through, so the action is driven forward by Nikki reluctantly returning to Murania – but bringing Martha (Phyllis Dare) with him. Once back in Murania, Vanescu plots against him; a reprise of the King vs Prime Minister scenario in *Glamorous Night*. As King, he has a duty to marry and produce an heir, so the beautiful, virginal, Princess Cristiane (Vanessa Lee) is chosen for him.

Nikki remains loyal to Martha, but Cristiane, pretending to be a maid (this is before the two have been properly introduced) seduces Nikki and becomes pregnant by him. He marries her and they have a son, but it is an essentially loveless marriage as he prefers the older Martha to his stunning young bride. There is political agitation stirred up by the Prime Minister, who dislikes Nikki's interest in public affairs, and at one point a mob of peasants break into Martha's house, where Nikki is visiting, and they are only saved by the quick thinking of Cristiane, who has also called by, and whose presence defuses the situation.

Eventually Nikki is persuaded that the best interest of the

Ivor with Phyllis Monkman, Beatrice Lillie and Olive Gilbert

country will be served if the Crown skips a generation and passes to his handsome teenage son, so he abdicates, and returns to Paris and Martha. The boy is crowned in a spectacular ceremony, set in the national cathedral.

Ivor's coronation song is one of his best pieces, sounding

Ivor and Vanessa Lee enjoy an offstage hug, King's Rhapsody,

as stirring, and authentic, as anything by William Walton. After the boy is crowned and the Cathedral empties, Cristiane, now Queen Mother, suspecting that Nikki might have slipped into the service, leaves a white rose as a symbol of her love. Nikki, in black, picks it up, sinks gracefully to his knees on the altar steps, and bows his head as the curtain falls.

As the curtain fell the audience rose, and the show was confirmed as yet another Novello triumph, with one magazine wearily commenting that to the two supposedly inevitable things in life – Death and Taxes – should be added a third – the inevitable success of a Novello first night. Even Noël Coward like it, but couldn't resist a sideswipe as well: 'The show was much better than anything he has done before. It had a few embarrassing moments and was, as usual, too long, but Zena Dare was excellent...Vanessa Lee absolutely enchanting; a lovely voice, terrific looks and can act. Terrific ovation at the end. We dined at the Ivy...'

King's Rhapsody was able to strike a blow against the prevailing wisdom that only American musicals would be both popular and profitable, and it did so partly because of the usual factors of Ivor's stage presence, his star-studded cast (Ivor wore, as part of his royal uniform, a star that had belonged to Edmund Kean) the lavishness of the set, the special dances, the blend of comedy and romance, but also because of a consistently well-made score.

Vanessa Lee's big number was 'Some Day my Heart Will Awake', which stopped the show every night; Olive Gilbert was given 'Fly Home Little Heart'. Phyllis Dare sang a comedy number resuscitated from *Arc de Triomphe*, 'The Mayor of Perpignan'. Of the other songs 'If This Were Love' is gently lyrical, 'Take Your Girl' is rumbustious and fun, but 'The Gates of Paradise' is one of Ivor's best – romantic but rousing at the same time.

Perchance to Dream had attracted audiences because people wanted an antidote to six years of war. By the time *King's Rhapsody* came out they were sick of four years of post-war Austerity. The popular response to the brief blaze of colour and pageantry that Princess Elizabeth's wedding to Prince Philip had produced in 1947, convinced Ivor – who loved Royal weddings and, even better, coronations – there was still a market for Royalty, even – or especially – in Attlee's Britain.

His commercial sense had been confirmed when, between the two musicals, he had written *We Proudly Present* (Duke of York's Theatre, 2 May 1947), a typically generous gesture towards Peter Daubeny, a young actor whose career was ruined when he lost an arm in action in Italy. Ivor took him to dinner at the Savoy and offered to write a play for him – his acting days might have been ended by the war, but if he wanted a career in the theatre, he could have one as a producer.

Ivor's health deteriorated during the run of *King's Rhapsody*, and he had to take several weeks sick leave. At the end of 1950, after more than a year of playing Nikki every week, he decided to have a long rest in his holiday home in Montego Bay, Jamaica.

As usual he took a gang of friends with him, and the weather was appropriately warm and inviting – though there was a hairy moment on the aircraft on the way there, and as the aeroplane carrying the cream of British musical theatre bounced and bumped its way through severe air turbulence, he wrote, on the back of an envelope, a gentle, elegiac song called, appropriately, 'Pray For Me.'

The weeks in the sun deepened his tan but did nothing for the underlying ill health that was to dog him for the remaining few months of his life. Though he endeavoured to be on good form for his neighbour and unlikely friend, Lord Beaverbrook, he lacked the same carefree joie de vivre, the careless rapture of earlier years. When he returned to London in freezing rain he was met by MacQueen Pope, who was concerned at his evident ill health. Ivor shrugged it off as just a cold, but he had only a few weeks to live.

He gave himself a rare night off from *King's Rhapsody* to attend another, and the last, of his first nights, this time a light musical he had written for Cicely Courtneidge, called *Gay's the Word*.

Far removed from the vast extravaganzas of Drury Lane, this was a small scale musical (though still using a larger cast than many 'major' modern ones) about a retired music hall singer, Gay Daventry – hence the somewhat unfortunate title, which has nothing to do with sexual orientation although the word was being used with its current meaning by this time, and Ivor, with his penchant for camp alternative titles for his shows, may have been playing a private practical joke on the public.

Gay Daventry runs a drama school, which seems harmless enough, but she becomes involved both in one last hurrah of a musical and a gang of smugglers. The juvenile leads were played by Lizbeth Webb and Thorley Walters, whose best number was 'A Matter of Minutes', but the show belonged to Cicely Courtneidge.

Ivor wrote the show (Alan Melville provided the sharp, witty lyrics) to rescue her failing career – which it did, giving her a new lease of professional life for another decade. He provided two major songs for her. The best known, which became her signature tune, is 'Vitality'. Something of a list song, it is a tribute to the Edwardian stars whom Ivor, Ciceley, and the middle aged and elderly in their audience, would have remembered vividly, and with affection.

In 'Vitality' Gay contrasts the old troupers, who performed live, without needing to use any 'microphone tricks' to get their songs across. The song works very well in its context, but by far the best song in *Gay's the Word* was a much quieter one, a reflective number called 'If Only He'd Looked My Way.'

The song describes an Edwardian dandy – 'masses of black hair' and, in the buttonhole of his evening jacket, a white gardenia - 'he always wore a white gardenia'. This was a might-have been romance that Gay wistfully recalls for the younger generation. It would lend itself equally well to being sung in a smoky night-club or bar at three in the morning, by a chanteuese with a hint of Marlene Dietrich's sexy, husky, voice. Marianne Faithful, who recorded 'Mad About the Boy' on the *20th Century Blues* album – of Coward songs sung by modern stars – would be ideal. This is, of course, one of the problems with Ivor – his songs are not given fresh interpretations and brought before a new audience in the same way as those of Coward, Porter, or Rodgers and Hammerstein.

At the first night of *Gay's the Word* (16 February 1951) at the Saville Theatre, Shaftesbury Avenue, Ivor sat in a box, looking elegant and handsome in a dinner jacket, but battling a dangerously high temperature. At the curtain call the audience directed their applause at him as much as at the cast, and he was forced (if that's the right word for someone who lived on public displays of affection) to stand to acknowledge the ovation. Characteristically, even at this moment of personal triumph, he gestured to Cicely Courtneidge and told the public that all their applause should be for her.

Ivor receives some puzzling news on the phone...

Critical response to *Gay's the Word* varied. The *Daily Express* asked a rhetorical question: 'How long can Ivor Novello keep turning out theatre-hugging hits? Last night Britain's top showman gave the answer...A new trick was wanted: the old dog has learned one. How long can he go on? As long as he can do as well as this'.

One of the points of *Gay's the Word*, as the *Daily Express* seemed to pick up, was that it was a new show; a break from the past. Not only

was it on a wholly different scale from Ivor's larger musicals, it poked fun at them as well, with one song – 'Ruritania' – spoofing Ivor's past taste for rows of singing hussars and Austro-Hungarian uniforms.

The *Evening Standard* assured its readers that 'No Richard Rodgers, Cole Porter or Irving Berlin can unthrone him.' Kenneth Tynan, in the Spectator, was characteristically critical: 'If I do not enjoy this, it is probably because I have memories of an aunt who did much the same thing at church socials' while the most virulent, yet even-handed, critic was Noël Coward, who saw it several months after the opening night:

'The worst in the theatre in the evening – *Gay's the Word...* stinking with bad taste and the intermixed vulgarity of Ivor and Alan Melville. Cicely Courtneidge a miracle of vitality and hard work, but, oh dear, with that horrible stuff to do. It was rapturously received by a packed house.'

The reception was confirmation of Ivor's continued ability, after two decades, to judge the public taste, and to know how far he could veer from his usual formula. No other composers would have had the self-awareness, and the fundamental modesty, to mock themselves and the shows that had made them rich, particularly with one such still running in the West End. That Ivor was able to do this through a musical that was leaner, fresher, and more modern than any of its predecessors, suggests that though his days as a matinee idol were drawing to a close, he was far from running out of artistic ability or box office appeal.

Meanwhile, he returned to the Palace Theatre and *King's Rhapsody*, overcoming his illness as he had overcome all previous obstacles, from Mam's attempts to keep him off the stage to a vicious judge's determination to make an example of him precisely because it was on the stage that earned his living. He had once told a reporter, when asked, among other supposedly searching questions, how he would like to die: 'I should like to make an enchanting curtain speech at the end of a wildly successful first night, and – to the sounds of cheers and applause – drop gracefully dead. If possible, before the curtain falls.' He came close to achieving it.

On the evening of 5 March he played Nikki in *King's Rhapsody* as usual, took the customary curtain calls, then went back to the flat in the Rolls and had a light supper. When he wasn't going out to the Ivy, the Caprice, or the Café de Paris, he like to go home, change, have a light supper of scrambled eggs on toast, then stay up until the early hours, unwinding over a game of canasta, or just chatting to friends.

On this occasion he was joined by Tom Arnold, his producer, and Ivor offered him champagne. Earlier that evening Ivor had complained of chest pains, but he was feeling better now. He liked to drink, usually white wine, but only a glass or

A reminder of Ivor in his prime, 1928

two with any meal. He loathed the loss of dignity and self control than went with being drunk, and drunken actors (not unknown in the theatre) were one of the few things that roused him to public displays of anger. Robert Newton, who

Ivor (right) relaxing at the Café de Paris with Tyrone Power and Linda Christian

appeared in *I Lived With You* was, once, drunk on stage; Ivor never forgave him.

This evening he had great difficulty opening the champagne bottle; his strength seemed to have deserted him, and he began to feel weak. Making a joke out of an unpleasant situation, as usual, he smashed the neck of the champagne bottle against a table, acting as if he were launching a ship. (Purists will note that it is the bottom rather than the top of the bottle that is smashed against a ship's hull, but this was a theatrical flat, not a shipyard). The champagne simply exploded over the floor, so Tom Arnold opened another one, then they had a light meal together. Afterwards, Ivor went to bed, but began to feel unwell again. Bobbie Andrews, who lived in the flat with Ivor, called a doctor, and alerted Olive Gilbert, who came up from her flat on the floor below. By the time the doctor arrived, Ivor was dying, and knew it. He was examined, and given a brandy, but there was no point in moving him. He was comfortable, at home and with two of the people to whom he was closest. The death itself was quick and easy – he gave a deep sigh and passed away. He was only fifty-eight years old.

Ivor in his later years…hints of mortality but the glamour's still there

AFTER THE BALL

Despite the unsocial hour – about two in the morning – Bobbie began telephoning Ivor's friends: as anyone who has lost a partner will know, dealing with the practical arrangements helps, in the immediate aftermath, in coming to terms with the death itself.

The news of his death was the first item on radio news headlines and on the front pages of the newspapers. Brook Williams, the son of Emlyn Williams, another Welsh boy who made good in the West End, remembers how the news of Ivor's death stunned his parents and their house guests, in a way that one would have expected only in the case of a very close member of the family or one of the major Royals. This sense of shock was felt not just in the theatre world but among the general public as well. He was not in the prime of life, but he was still a relatively young man, at the height of his artistic success, performing in his best (and most profitable) show to date, with his earlier musicals still regularly performed and his new hit, *Gay's the Word*, suggesting that he was even more versatile than had been previously supposed.

He was also working on a new show, to be set in his native Wales, with him playing the role of a choirmaster – a complete return to his roots. Some tentative work that he had done on a show set in Wales, *Lily of the Valley*, was completed by others (including Christopher Hassall) and called *Valley of Song*, but without Ivor's stage presence, let alone his normal amount of work on the songs, it was distinctly below par, and cannot be counted as part of his work.

His popularity may have been limited to these islands, and to South Africa, which he had conquered with charm during his

191

1947 tour, but it was all the stronger in a society which, at that time, was far less cosmopolitan than today, and for which he represented a British personification of the most romantic and exciting elements of Abroad.

That he had been a national favourite for nearly thirty-seven years made his sudden disappearance all the more shocking. He had been known to everyone, from his closest friends to complete strangers, as Ivor; for he radiated a friendliness and warmth – while retaining his privacy, and dignity – that no other celebrity ever matched.

In an age long before the casual familiarity and pretended intimacy between media celebrities and the general public, he was the only major star, with the exception, perhaps, of Gracie Fields or George Formby, whom everyone felt they knew. Unlike those two, however, his 'next door' qualities and approachability were complemented by a glamour, and by a physical beauty and stylishness that neither Fields nor Formby had a hope of approaching. Indeed, their particular appeal was based on their lack of it. Additionally, at the time of his death, he had been a household name for nearly twenty years longer than they had.

Noël Coward was distraught, though not enough to avoid criticism:

'A shocking and sad day because Ivor is suddenly dead. He died late last night or early this morning of a heart attack. The first intimation I had was from the *Daily Express* asking me to write about him. This I did not understand, as the cable said nothing about his death. The other cables came...felt awful. Shall miss him very much because, in spite of his plays and his acting, I was very fond of him...'

The newspapers played up this sense of Ivor's glamorous lifestyle. The reports tell us as much about the period as they do about his reputation. Food rationing was still in force, for example, so when the *Daily Express* wanted to convey the luxury in which Ivor lived, they showed a photo of his desk at the flat, handily labelling, for the benefit of their more short-sighted (and poor) readers, three extravagant items: a bottle of champagne, a large bar of chocolate, and an orange!

The *Evening Standard* ran a thoughtful tribute by Beverley Baxter, M.P., who recalled how, only a couple of weeks earlier,

Ivor, looking fatherly with Vanessa Lee

in his very positive review of *Gay's the Word*, he had written that it was high time that Ivor had received an honour for his unique contribution to British musical theatre. As he now ruefully remarked, it was too late for that, and all that could be hoped was that his public would remember him.

His prison sentence, brief though it was, had put paid to any hope of a long-overdue recognition of his contribution to popular culture, but his public were determined that though he had missed out on a knighthood, he would get a quasi-Royal funeral. There was none of the hysteria that Valentino's funeral had seen

Being a gorgeous, wealthy matinée idol could be so tiring…

in 1926, but then Ivor was nearly sixty rather than in his thirties, and this was a British crowd rather than an American one, in an era when grief – and the suddenness of Ivor's death had increased the sense of shock and loss – was born with stoicism and restraint, not explosions of emotion.

Bobbie Andrews, typically, brought his brand of waspish humour to the preparations for the funeral service. An actress friend had telephoned him in floods of tears, unsure whether she would be able to cope with the event – she hated funerals. Exasperated, Bobbie snapped that Ivor wasn't very keen on them either, and was only going to this one because he didn't have a say in the matter.

His ashes were buried at the crematorium, and are marked by a small lilac tree in front of one of the numerous chapels on the site. Nearby, in a high alcove under the cloisters there is a teracotta bust of Ivor (in profile, of course), with the words 'we shall not see his like again'. There are four other memorials to him in London – a blue plaque by the door to his flat at 11 Aldwych, a plaque to his memory (illustrated by his profile) at St Paul's Cathedral, a wooden memorial plaque at the actor's church, St Paul's, Covent Garden, which refers to his kindness, and a bust, by Clemence Dane, in the Theatre Royal, Drury Lane.

Of the many private tributes that Ivor received, that of Zena Dare, his stage mother both in *Proscenium* and *King's Rhapsody*, was the most poignant, remembering how he would say: "Oh, this really is a lovely play" as if he had been watching someone else's for the first time, rather than performing in his one of his own.

Of the public, the plaque at St Paul's is the most interesting. Not for itself, but for what it tells us about Ivor's reputation. Douglas Bader's presence, and admiration, is a mark of how effectively Ivor's music caught the British public's moods during the two world war that the nation had to endure. 'Keep the Home Fires Burning' had been an alternately comforting and rousing anthem for troops and civilian relatives and sweethearts alike in the First World War, while 'We'll Gather Lilacs' had expressed a generation's hopes for peace during the Second. In between these two landmarks, Ivor's music had entertained servicemen and their families on leave during both conflicts, and *The Dancing Years*, in particular, brought a welcome evening of escapism, tinged with defiance, amid the horrors of nearly six years of Total War.

It was for this extraordinary achievement rather than for his entertaining but ephemeral West End comedies, or for the numerous films that had stirred so many teenage hearts, that he was honoured at St Paul's, and the honour had come about through public pressure, and was partly financed by a fund-raising concert at Drury Lane. It had taken twenty-three years to get him acknowledged by the Establishment, but the popularity that had made it necessary to have loudspeakers to relay the memorial service at St Martin's in the Fields to the huge crowds in Trafalgar Square, had finally won recognition – next to another popular composer, Sir Arthur Sullivan.

It has been Ivor's musicals rather than his plays or films that have kept his memory alive. The tragedy is that, despite the gallant efforts of John Hanson and a handful of others, professional performances of Ivor's shows dwindled rapidly within a few years of his death, and his music, today, is best known in concert form, on programmes like Radio 2's *Friday Night is Music Night*, or in performances, concert or staged, by amateur operatic companies, usually playing to very good houses, as there is still, pace the big producers, a market for Ivor's shows.

The problem, for Ivor's wider reputation, is that they are hardly ever performed professionally. Gallant versions (such as Buxton Opera House's performance of *The Dancing Years* in 1992, and Harrow Light Opera's concert version of *The Dancing Years* and *King's Rhapsody* in 1993) are no replacement for a full-scale West End revival. The usual explanation for this lack of interest among producers is that Ivor's shows require such enormous casts (over 80 on stage at one point in *Careless Rapture*) and expensive sets and costumes, if they are to be presented to full advantage, that they are simply uneconomic.

The obvious solution is for a subsidised organisation to mount a Novello show. This has so far failed to happen, with the National (which is, in general, a superb platform for British talent and world drama) preferring to perform American revivals – most of which would be as appropriately done by commercial producers as the National. The argument in favour of American musicals is usually that they are better known, and more popular, than anything by Novello – or any other British composer, for that matter.

This is a self-perpetuating argument, and the refusal of managements to back a Novello revival is the main reason why he is relatively unknown. He also faces the unspoken assumption that his work is of interest only to the old, and the other assumption – born, one suspects, of a lack of knowledge – that his work is lushly romantic and limited to operetta – a poor man's Lehàr.

As this book and its predecessors show, and as study of his work demonstrates, the truth is vastly different. In order to break through the resistance to his musicals, he needs to be seen as chic again, for the first time in half a century. This is more likely to come about through an appreciation of his work as a film star (in that cinema is more fashionable than theatre) or as a glamorous personality, like Noël Coward, than as a composer, though his music is his artistic legacy.

The number of people who worked with Ivor has, naturally, been reduced to a handful. Mary Ellis, who died in 2003, officially aged 102 but actually 105, lived for many years, until shortly before her death, in a flat in Eaton Square. Her funeral, in Chelsea, was an understated affair (all her contemporaries and most of her friends and colleagues up to 20 years younger than her having already died) made all the more poignant by the tiny size of her coffin. When I interviewed her in 1992 she looked at least twenty years younger than her age, and had perfect recall of her years with Ivor, taking me through her photo albums and reminiscing about the shows which it illustrated. Sitting with her I reminded myself that I was talking to a woman who had sung at the New York Met during the First World War – an extraordinary sensation in a Belgravia drawing room in the early 1990s.

A further bridge to the past was opened when she saw me out. Pointing across the landing to the door of another flat, she said that that was where Vivien Leigh had spent her last years, dying there, of tuberculosis, in 1967. She had been a great friend of Ivor's, from when they had acted together in *The Happy Hypocrite* at His Majesty's Theatre in 1936, until Ivor's death. As with many of the beautiful women for whom he wrote roles in his plays and musicals, he had an extraordinary empathy with her, and though he got on with Laurence Olivier, he was, essentially, Vivien's friend.

Shortly after seeing Mary Ellis I met Roma Beaumont, whose career on stage had ended shortly after Ivor's death. She, too, had vivid memories of her times with Ivor and unselfconsciously stressed his kindness and generosity. She herself radiated niceness, and the afternoon spent at her home, and walking on the nearby Heath (she insisted on walking me not just to the garden gate, but across the

Heath to the bus stop) was one of the most relaxing and pleasant that I can remember.

A similar atmosphere of niceness (a word one was taught in English lessons at school never to use, but which ideally suits certain atmospheres and occasions) pervades Ivor's old country home, Redroofs. After a brief and unsuccessful spell as a retirement home for actors – a sort of Berkshire version of Denville Hall – it became, and remains, a theatre school.

When I visited Redroofs Theatre School, I was met by the proprietor whose name, June Rose, seems perfect for a Novello heroine - which is what, in effect she is. Keeping the house alive, and filled with young talent, she has a strong sense of its past, and an enormous admiration for Ivor, whom she has commemorated through the Novello Theatre, a nearby building where the drama school students learn their craft.

There is also, appropriately, a tiny theatre in Redroofs itself. There is such a thing as 'atmospheres' in houses, and Redroofs, which was a famously happy place during the twenty plus years that Ivor lived there, has the most immediately welcoming and peaceful atmosphere of any building I have ever been in. Even if one discounts the inevitable attraction of a place one knows to have been enjoyed by someone one admires, there is still something remarkable about Redroofs.

It is largely for this reason, as well as for his own memories of the place, that led Gordon Duttson, Ivor's last private secretary, to leave his collection of published and unpublished photos of Ivor, his shows, his homes, friends and entourage to June Rose and the Redroofs Theatre School. He was at Redroofs, too, for the unveiling of a plaque to Ivor by the Ivor Novello Appreciation Bureau, a dedicated and knowledgeable group of enthusiasts who themselves own a considerable collection of Ivor memorabilia.

Of Ivor's films, *The Lodger* is the only one to get a fairly frequent outing (thanks to Hitchcock's reputation rather than Ivor's). It has been shown on Channel Four Television, and has had numerous airings, accompanied by a pianist, at the National Film Theatre on the South Bank. In Spring 1999 it was featured in a series of Hitchcock films shown at the Barbican Arts Centre to mark the director's centenary.

Ivor, made up and ready to go in King's Rhapsody

More memorably, *The Lodger* was screened, outdoors, at the National Theatre, in July 2004. The film was projected onto the exterior wall of the theatre, facing the Thames, and could be clearly seen not just from 'Theatre Square' but from Waterloo Bridge and indeed from the Savoy Hotel, where Ivor had been a regular in his youth, and where I was staying that night. The overall effect was something like a scene out of *Cinema Paradiso*.

The rest of Ivor's film work remains relatively unknown - to the general public, at least - though recognition of its importance was made when a still from *I Lived With You* was used for the cover of Professor Jeffrey Richards' characteristically entertaining and informative book The Unknown 1930s: An Alternative History of British Cinema 1929-1939.

Ivor's unsuccessful 1932 talkie remake of *The Lodger* was mentioned (by Maggie Smith's character, a scarcastic countess) in Robert Altman's film *Gosford Park* (2001), an elegant murder mystery set in an English country house weekend in the early 1930s. The film has Ivor (played by Jeremy Northam) as a major character and many of his songs feature on the soundtrack. In one particularly striking scene he is at the piano, playing a selection of his songs for the assorted houseguests, most of whom ignore him and chatter among themselves, while the servants (representing the general public who were to flock to his musicals in the 1930s, 40s and 50s) secretly listen, enthralled. The film, which deservedly won an Oscar for screenwriter Julian Fellowes, introduced Ivor to an American audience, most of whom had never heard of him before.

Despite this, the shameful neglect of Ivor's major musical theatre productions by the National Theatre, already referred to in this chapter, was continued and reinforced when Nicholas Hytner firmly turned down, at a press conference, any possibility of his staging a revival of any Novello production. It was all the more refreshing, then, that one of the country's leading musicians, Mark Elder - Music Director of the Hallé orchestra in Manchester - chose to programme a concert of Novello music at the Bridgewater Hall in April 2005.

The evening, with a script by myself , and narrated with authority and panache by Simon Callow, featured Janis Kelly (soprano) and Barry Banks (tenor), and was conducted by Mark Elder - who also made his stage singing debut with a stylish rendition of 'And Her Mother Came Too'. Its success proved the continued appeal of Ivor's work, provided it is presented professionally and with the level of artistry and enthusiasm that the original work received.

The hope that some sort of Novello revival might therefore be finally underway was further boosted not long after with the announcement that Sir Cameron Mackintosh was to rename the Strand Theatre, in the West End, the Novello - following a programme of refurbishment in the summer of 2005. At the same time it was announced that another of his London theatres, the Albery, was to become the Noël Coward.

The renaming of the Strand was particularly inspired, as not only was Ivor closely associated with the theatre, in that he had lived above it for nearly forty years, but the Strand was an undistinguished and misleading name - it is actually located, not in the Strand but in the Aldwych, separated from the theatre of that name by the Waldorf Hotel (officially, at the time of writing, the Waldorf Hilton).

Perhaps, and at last, given this remarkable endorsement of his place in British theatre history, we will finally see a producer/director stage a revival of one of Ivor's many musicals. There have been a number of small scale shows featuring his music and telling his story, but it is time to see *Glamorous Night* or *King's Rhapsody* back on stage. The logical venue would be the Coliseum , which in 2005 staged a revival of (surprise, surprise) an American Musical: Bernstein's *On The Town*. This was an interesting ·production made memorable by Stephen Mears' choreography, but English National Opera should have staged a British musical rather than an American one. Why have a subsidised company and theatre if it only stages the sort of work that can be readily seen in the commercial West End?

Whatever the future in terms of revivals of his shows, his contribution to past British popular culture is marked by the existence of the Ivor Novello Awards (which celebrated their 50th anniversary in 2005) and, now, by the fact that a major London playhouse, in the heart of the West End, bears his name. Other major theatrical or cinematic figures are often cited in comparison with rising stars – 'the new Laurence Olivier', 'the new Clark Gable' – but we are never again likely to have an individual with Ivor's combination of looks and talent. To provide an equivalent range of natural gifts and artistic achievement in recent years would have required Keanu Reeves to have complemented his film career with a string of plays (as writer and leading actor) followed by his having composed and starred in all of Andrew Lloyd Webber's musicals. An enjoyable idea, but, clearly, a fantasy. As Ivor's memorial at Golders Green rightly says, we shall not see his like again.

FURTHER READING

Balcon, M *Twenty Years of British Films, 1925-45* (Falcon Press, 1947)

Cook, Pam *Gainsborough Pictures* (Cassell, 1997)

Courtneidge, Cicely *Cicely* (Hutchinson, 1953)

Curtis, A *The Rise and Fall of the Matinee Idol* (Weidenfeld and Nicolson, 1974)

Davies, Rhys *The Painted King* (Heinemann, 1954)

Ellis, Mary *Those Dancing Years* (John Murray, 1982)

Harding, J *Ivor Novello* (W H Allen, 1987)

Hassall, Christopher *Edward Marsh* (Longmans, 1959)

MacQueen Pope, W *Ivor Novello* (Heinemann, 1951)

Morley, Sheridan *Gladys Cooper* (Heinemann, 1979)

Noble, P *Ivor Novello* (Falcon Press, 1951)

Richards, J *The Unknown 1930s* (I.B. Tauris, 1998)

Rose, R *Perchance to Dream* (Leslie Frewin, 1974)

Wilson, S *Ivor* (Michael Joseph, 1975)

PICTURE CREDITS

The author and publisher wish to express their thanks to the following sources of illustrative material and /or permission to reproduce it. They will make proper acknowledgements in future editions in the event that any omissions have occurred.

The photographs on pages 24 and 46 (by Edmund Harrington) are courtesy of the National Portrait Gallery Photographic Archive. The Photographs on pages 179, 180 and 199 are courtesy of the PA Photo News agency. The photographs on pages 132 and 146/7 are courtesy of the Stoll Moss Theatre Collection. All other photographs and illustrations are courtesy of the Mander and Mitchenson Theatre Collection.

INDEX

Works by or featuring Novello appear under title; all songs are by Novello. IN indicates Novello.